RED FLAGS TO REDEMPTION

NO LONGER TRYING TO SPARE YOUR FEELINGS

───── AN INTERACTIVE POETRY JOURNAL ─────

LAUREL E. MOOREHEAD-SUAREZ

Copyright © 2024 Croix Management Group

All rights reserved. No part of this book may be reproduced, stored in a retrievel system in any form or by any means, electronic, mechanical, photocopying, recording, or otherwise, without written permission of the publisher, except where permitted by law.

To request permissions, contact the publisher at info@croixmanagementgroup.com.

ISBN: 979-8-9916469-9-4

Croix Management Group
www.laurelthewriter.com

DEDICATION

I wrote this for me.

Hey there!

To be honest, this book started as something I compiled for myself. These words are the result of my life's journey—both planned and spontaneous encounters, stories from strangers, friends, and loved ones, and my observations of the relationships around me. They are raw, honest expressions, some born from my own triggering moments and steps in the healing process as I move toward wholeness. I hope you find pieces of your story here—whether it's a verse that resonates with your heart or a line that offers comfort when you need it most.

I dedicate this book to you and to everyone who has ever felt misunderstood, embarrassed, or not quite ready to fully stand in their truth. If a poem or verse speaks to you, I encourage you to share it and tag me @IAmFlawfullyUnapologetic. Let's connect through these words because healing happens together.

With love and light,

Laurel E. **Moorehead**-Suarez
@IAmFlawfullyUnapologetic

N.L.C.

This interactive poetry journal includes reflection questions, discussion prompts, and plenty of space for scribbling your thoughts.

CONTENTS

COLOR BLIND BY CHOICE

COLORBLIND BY CHOICE	11
RED FLAG: KNOW IT WHEN YOU SEE IT	15
LIFE AND LOVE IN DARK VERSES	19
WHEN YING MET YANG	20
THE FIRST WOUND	23
HE WAS BREASTFED TOO LONG	26
MIDDLE FINGER	29
TOXIC JUICE	31
GASLIGHT'S FLICKER	33
HAVE YOU SEEN THE BUTTERFLIES?	37
ROLE PLAY	39
MOMENTARY MADNESS	41
ALONE TOGETHER	45
TRUE LIES	47
DECEPTION OF SELF	49
SIS! YOU MISUNDERSTOOD	53
ADDICTED TO BEING CHOSEN	59
REPAIR SHOP BLUES	62
AN AFTERTHOUGHT	63
HEALING METAPHORS	65
SILENT EROSION:	67
SABOTAGE SHENANIGANS	69
LOOK AT YOU, BEING YOUR OWN HUSBAND	72
TIGHT ROPES AND EGGSHELLS	77
THE COLORS OF A MOCKERY	79
HER LIGHT, HIS ENVY	81
EMBARRASSED ISOLATION	83

PIECES TO PEACE

PIECES TO PEACE	95
SHEDDING IS HEALING	97
GRACE	98
FORGIVE AND FORGET	102
I'VE LEARNED, I'VE LEARNED	103
THE COST OF QUIET ACCEPTANCE	106
SINS OF HER FATHER	107
DILUTED ESSENCE	108
FREEFALL - NO ANCHOR	113
AM I THE DRAMA?	115
MOTHER'S CHAINS	117
BEYOND FEAR AND MUCK	121
SOUL ARCHITECT	123
DON'T RUN! LET THE SCARS GUIDE YOU	129
ILLUSION VS DELUSION	131
THE SHACKLES OF LOYALTY	133
WHEN HEARTS DON'T ALIGN	137
GRIEF: THE UNINVITED GUEST	141
LOSS: WORLD OFF ITS AXIS	144
NOTHING FOR YOU, EVERYTHING FOR ME	145
BLOCKED BLESSINGS	147
STIRRING THE POT	151
THE HEALING CYCLE	155

SHE FINALLY WOKE THE FUCK UP

THE SHIFT	163
A MESSAGE	164
CLARITY'S RELEASE	165
WASTING TIME	167
GONE BEFORE I LEFT	169
REMEMBER AND FORGIVE	170
BREAKING MOTHER'S CHAINS	175
NON-NEGOTIABLE	177
FLIRTING OR RAISED RIGHT?	181
MY DEAREST NEXT LIFETIME LOVE	182
MY SOUL'S PROMISE TO ME	186

COLOR BLIND BY CHOICE

COLOR BLIND BY CHOICE

Blinking signals, vibrant and clear,
You waved your red flags. I pretended not to see.
I pretended not to feel my gut screaming at me.
Blindly, I reached for my crayons, intent on a fix,
Coloring over the warnings, blending green into the mix.
How could anger find me, when the truth was so plain?
You were an open book of storms; I chose to see beautiful rain.

Each flag you hoisted, high and unfurled,
Was a twisted truth, a map to your world.
I painted over the red, with shades so serene,
Turning warnings into cute love notes, smothered in green.
In my array of denial, I found comfort in playing my part
Ignoring your actions, I recolored my heart.

Now, here in the quiet aftermath of my choice,
I ponder the colors, and the times I muted your voice.
For how can I fault you, when at every decree,
You showed me your true shades, but I chose not to see.

REFLECTIONS & REVELATIONS

DATE:

Journal Reflection:

- What personal experiences come to mind when reading this poem?
- Have there been times when you chose to overlook red flags in a relationship?
- How do you think ignoring these signals affected the outcome?

Discussion Questions:

- Why do we sometimes choose to focus on the positives in a relationship, even when faced with clear warning signs?
- In what ways do we 'color over the warnings' in our daily lives or relationships?
- What could be the impact of trusting our gut more often?

_____
_____
_____
_____
_____
_____
_____
_____
_____

RED FLAG:
KNOW IT WHEN YOU SEE IT

Do you hear that?
Those voices in your head as they start to rise,
Tiny doubts and questions, hidden in your eyes.
A smile that seems too guarded, laughter feels restrained,
In the early days of love, ignoring signs of future pain.

When words that once were gentle, stab without a cause.
When promises are broken, without a hint of pause.
When jealousy runs rampant, cloaked as deep concern.
And trust begins to falter, vessels it will burn.

Inconsistencies in stories, truths that come undone.
Gaslighting confusions, leaving you stunned and spun.
Isolation from your loved ones, friends kept at bay,
Controlling where you go, dictating what you say.

Your worth feels undermined, belittled and erased.
Apologies that come too late, a bitter aftertaste.
When anger flares in flashes, and kindness feels too rare.
When walking on eggshells is your constant state of care.

Trust your instincts, the feelings that you hide.
Recognize the red flags, let them be your guide.
Seek a love that's pure and gentle, that brings you peace and light,
For you deserve the kind of love that lets you sleep peacefully at night.

REFLECTIONS & REVELATIONS

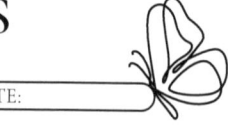

Journal Reflection:

- What emotions did this poem stir within you?
- Have you ever experienced or witnessed a relationship where these signs were present? How did it affect you?
- What do you think it means to "trust your instincts"? How has your intuition guided you in past relationships?

Discussion Questions:

- What's a red flag you ignored in the past that, looking back, was screaming at you?
- When did you realize it was time to walk away, and what was the final straw?
- Have you ever had that friend who's ignoring all the red flags, and how do you help (or do you even bother)?

_____
_____
_____
_____
_____
_____
_____
_____

LIFE AND LOVE IN DARK VERSES

One night before retiring,
to their separate beds, separate rooms, he asked of her,
"Why not pen tales of love's delight, of joyous' spree?"
Her silence lingered like the pause of a deer in headlights.
Her words born, were only filled with spite.
Long did she sit with pen in hand, her spirit sore,
Seeking in vain across this blighted, barren shore,
To capture sunlight, laughter's ease, in ink and prose,
Yet only burrowed sorrows her weary pen chose.

Each line she drew was steeped in pain, in rivers cried,
Of loveless moments, of dreams denied.
How could she write of love's sweet bloom
when all she knew were thorns that pricked and chilling gloom?

She responded...
Dearest Love:
Forgive me if I paint our world in shades of dark gray.
Though I try, the joyous tint in my ink slips far away.
My stories speak of life as felt, not as wished to be,
I hope you'll see my honesty in every verse and plea.

WHEN YING MET YANG

Ying marveled at how she had found her Yang,
a contrasting light that illuminated her world.
Opposite souls in a seamless blend,
Whispered love that would never end.
Yin's calm night to Yang's fierce day,
In their twilight dance, they found their way.
Attraction sparked, a flame so wild,
In their embrace, they crafted a child.
From one, they grew to a family tree,
Roots entwined for the world to see.
Their union, a tale of good times and cheer,
As months to years collided near.
But time, the thief, with silent tread,
Stole the harmony, left doom instead.

What once was whole now halved in strife,
The rift grew, cut like a knife.
Yang's fire burned a touch too bright,
Yin's peacefulness lost in night.
The balance tipped, the scales did sway,
And slowly, sadly, they frayed away.
Opposites still, once a perfect match.
Now parallel lines that no longer attach.
Divided they stand, a love once grand.
Scattered like stars, in a sky so bland.
A union of contrasts that forever soar,
Now a journal of good ole' stories,
hidden behind a basement door.

What once was whole now halved in strife,
The rift grew, cut like a knife.
Yang's fire burned a touch too bright,
Yin's peacefulness lost in night.
The balance tipped, the scales did sway,
And slowly, sadly, they frayed away.
Opposites still, once a perfect match.
Now parallel lines that no longer attach.
Divided they stand, a love once grand.
Scattered like stars, in a sky so bland.
A union of contrasts that forever soar,
Now a journal of good ole' stories,
hidden behind a basement door.

THE FIRST WOUND

The first time he called her a fat bitch,
She should have left him curled up in a ditch.
The first time he called her a stupid cunt,
She should have left all his shit out front.
His words, like daggers, pierced her heart,
Leaving her speechless, torn apart.
In an instant, love turned to regret,
Her joy faded to silent fret.
A sneer, a glare, harsh words that fly,
Left emotionally battered,
her spirit trembled, screaming to defy.
She questioned herself, "What did I do?"
Lost in confusion, without a damn clue.
The first wound cut deep, raw, and new,
His anger unwarranted, his rage untamed,
Leaving her helpless and feeling so ashamed.

REFLECTIONS & REVELATIONS

DATE:

Journal Reflection:

- How did this poem stir your emotions?
- Have you or someone you know faced similar emotional abuse?
- What early signs might show a relationship turning harmful, and how can you recognize them within yourself?
- How do shame and helplessness affect someone's ability to leave a toxic relationship, and what inner strength can help?

Discussion Questions:

- How do you recover from that first really painful moment in a relationship?
- What would you tell your younger self about recognizing verbal or emotional abuse?
- Have you ever stayed in a relationship too long after the first red flag?
- What kept you there?

_____
_____
_____
_____
_____
_____
_____

HE WAS BREASTFED TOO LONG

He was breastfed too long, clinging to the past,
A man in years, but a boy half-assed.
Dependent on others, unable to stand tall,
No backbone to lean on, destined to fall.

Spoiled by his mother, coddled with too much care,
Shielded from struggles, from burdens to bear.
In his mother's embrace, he lingered too long,
Now a man-sized bitch standing lost in a world, where he doesn't belong.

Choices evade him, he's literally stuck hard in place.
Fearful of failure, a dumbstruck look permanent on his face.

His mother's intentions, though loving and kind,
Have left him unready for life's trying grind.
Now he glides through life, looking for a wife,
Destroying souls, causing unnecessary strife.
His lack of know-how, common sense so sparse,
Leaves broken hearts and lives in abysmal disarray.

Watch out! He was breastfed too long,
Now a man-child's adrift, with no courage or care,
and only heaping bullshit to share!

REFLECTIONS & REVELATIONS

DATE:

Journal Reflection:

- How do you think being overly sheltered can impact someone's ability to face life's challenges?
- What role does personal responsibility play in growing into adulthood, and how can avoiding it affect relationships?

Discussion Questions:

- We've all dated the "man-child" at least once—what was your first clue?
- How much do you think a person's upbringing shapes their behavior in a relationship?

_____
_____
_____
_____
_____
_____
_____
_____
_____
_____
_____

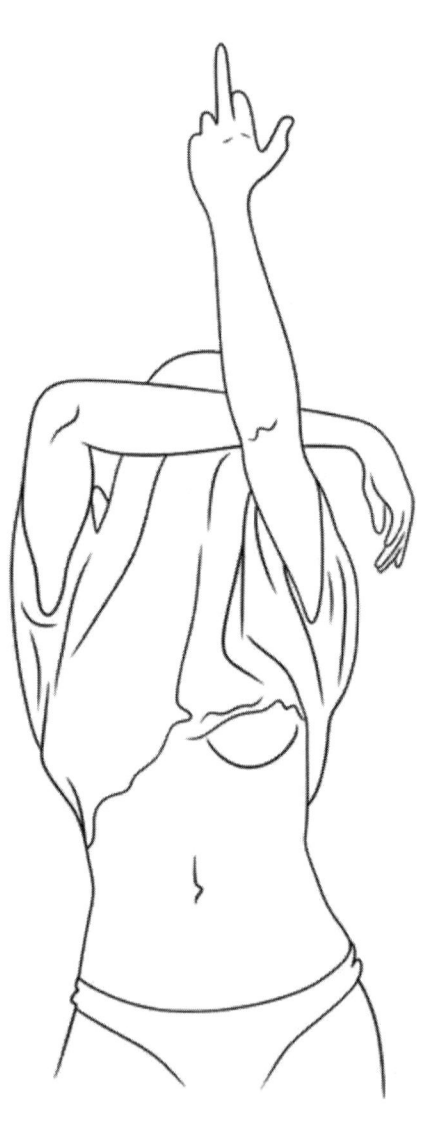

MIDDLE FINGER

Every time you walk by,
I feel the urge to raise my middle finger
behind your back, in a childish phase.

Corny and juvenile? Maybe.
But it feels so damn good to me,
A small rebellion that helps me feel such sweet glee.

TOXIC JUICE

TOXIC JUICE

He seduced her with whispers, a lover's deceit,
Promises bared, their hearts would meet.
In passion's embrace, their souls intertwined,
But what seemed like love, was a toxic bind.
Once they made love, a soul tie was formed,
His touch was a prison, his love a disguise,
Beneath the sheets, she laid dickmatized.
His tainted juice seeped into her pores,
Causing upheaval, opening hidden doors.
A storm of confusion, his poison spread wide,
Eroding her spirit, leaving nowhere to hide.
Toxic ties tightened, girth choking her light,
Bound by his sticky effervescence, she lost her fight.

GASLIGHT'S FLICKER

Did your voice grow faint,
As he whispered words, dipped in taint?
"You sound crazy," he said with a smirk,
Twisting truth into lies, a cruel, dark quirk.

"You're imagining things," his favorite refrain,
"I was just joking," yet it caused so much pain.
Shifting blame like a hula hoop's spin,
His words, a whirl, where did they begin?
"This is psychological warfare," it's plain to see,
"Denying my reality, what's left of me?"
Memory twisted, his words rewound,
Leaving you lost, in a gaslit gown.

"I never did that," he'd insist with ease,
Turning her mind into a tornado, wild with unease.
"You're so dramatic," he'd often proclaim,
Dimming her light, fueling the shame.
Confusion planted where trust once grew,
Each seed of doubt, imploding, gasoline now dripping all over you!

REFLECTIONS & REVELATIONS

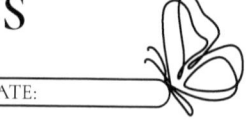
DATE:

Journal Reflection:

- Reflect on a time when you questioned your own feelings or experiences due to someone else's manipulation. How did you regain your clarity, and what did you learn from that experience?

Discussion Questions:

- Gaslighting is such a hot topic—have you ever experienced it, and how did you figure out what was going on?
- How do you regain trust in yourself after someone has made you question your own reality?

HAVE YOU SEEN THE BUTTERFLIES?

Where have the butterflies flown?
Tell me, where have they gone?
Gazing at you, I tremble, feeling strangely numb.
Your words, your voice, your thrusts deep within,
Now fail to touch the core of my soul, now wearing thin.

Where are the butterflies that danced even on our darkest days?
I promise I looked high and low, searched every silent cry,
But you, with your mean spirit, made their gentle spirits die.
Emptiness now swallows the air, a stifling, silent snare,
Each day a burial deep, and I, in mourning, despair.

Strangled were their wings, in the grip of your cold disdain,
Now gone forever; they may not return again.
The wings that fluttered, the rhythm they brought now lost,
Leaving behind a winter's sting, a stifling, grievous frost.
O lost butterflies, return, and fill this hollow heart.
Will this be the end, our paths eternally destined to be apart?

ROLE PLAY

This dimly lit room, where we play our parts,
I trace the lines not of love, but of art.
On the stage of our sheets, we rehearse our embrace,
Wishing it was love, not just a shared space.
I pretend to adore you, laugh at your jest,
While quietly plotting my emotional divest.
Each touch a script, each kiss a scene,
Where I act like you're king, and I, the queen.
Our bed—a theater of limp moans and sighs,
Costumes tossed aside under alibi skies.
I wish it were love that stirs my night's breeze,
Not the rehearsal for the day I'll leave.
For now, I'll play along in this shadowed ballet,
Dancing close, while my heart's miles away.
Wishing it was love making, genuine and true,
Instead of this play, where I pretend to love you.

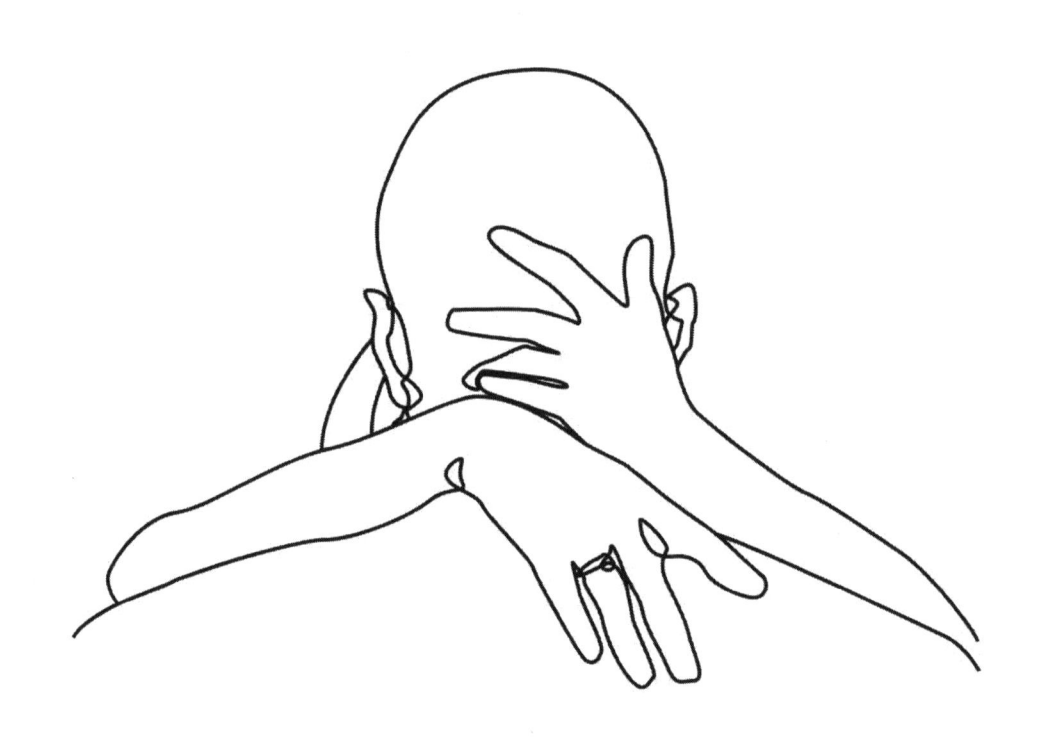

MOMENTARY MADNESS

She can't stand his ass!
She hates him, loathes him with a passion,
enkindling her blood on fire.
But damn, does he know how to push her buttons.

Deep breaths, trying to resist the magnetic pull,
But the weight of his body against hers owns her,
Dominating, yet somehow still asking for permission.

He enters slowly, teasingly, savoring every inch.
Her body betrays her, yet again, the quiet recesses awakening,
A simmering heat that only he can ignite.
Her heart races, a wild, chaotic rhythm that
matches the dance they've perfected.

Muscles tense and release, gripping him like a vice,
Guiding him, allowing him just as far as she wants
—no more, no less.
True power lies in this control, in the places unseen,
In the whispers of her deepest desires,
where she reigns supreme.

And then, just as the tension peaks, he retreats,
Leaving her breathless,
her body still tingling with the memory of his touch.
She still can't stand him,
But damn, she hopes to see him tomorrow.

REFLECTIONS & REVELATIONS

DATE:

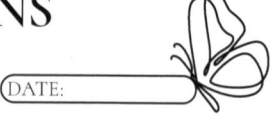

Journal Reflection:

- How does the tension between love and hate in this poem make you reflect on the complexity of your own relationships?
- What role does control and power play in desire, and how do these dynamics show up in your life?

Discussion Questions:

- Have you ever been in a relationship where the chemistry is off the charts, but everything else is a disaster?
- How do you separate physical attraction from emotional connection, or is it impossible sometimes?
- Do you think it's possible to be physically drawn to someone while still hating them a little on the inside?

_____

_____

_____

_____

_____

_____

_____

_____

_____

ALONE TOGETHER

Being titled as a significant other should have
made her feel cherished,
but instead, she was rendered invisible.
Her presence taken for granted like
an old piece of furniture in the corner of a room.

Every day, she painted a smile on her face,
A silent actor in the background of his life's play,
Where her lines were whispers lost in the wind.
He introduced her with pride but treated her with indifference,
As if her value was only as high as the esteem it brought him.

She was there, but not there—seen, yet unseen;
heard, but not listened to.
It's a strange limbo, loving someone who makes her feel
More alone than when she was single.
The promises exchanged became decorations,
pretty but dust-covered.
Every "I love you" belted,
lost in the polished cracks between them.

BLAH BLAH BLAH

TRUE LIES

He spins his tales with a silver tongue,
True lies woven, his songs unsung.
A master of stories, deceit his art,
In every tale, he plays the leading part.

When others bear witness, truth on their lips,
He crafts new lies with clever flips.
A star, a victor, in every scene,
His fabrications, so smooth, and clean.

Reality twisted, facts rearranged,
Memories blurred; details exchanged.
His storytelling makes one forget,
What really happened, a tangled net.
In the tales he weaves, he is never wrong,
A hero, a legend, always the same sing-song.
True lies flow, unending stream,
Reality lost, in his crafted dream.

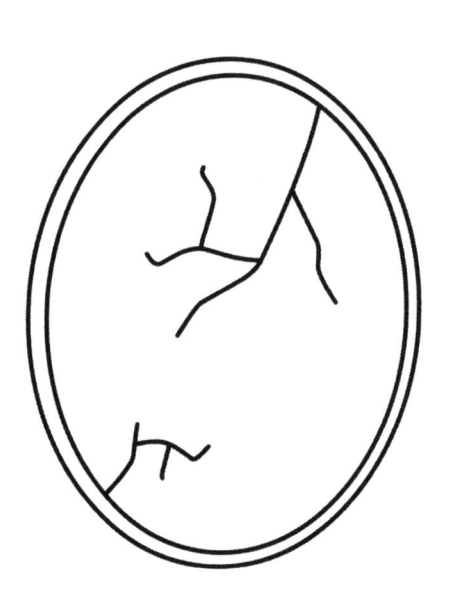

DECEPTION OF SELF

Sometimes, the most insidious form of self-deception is the brainwashing we inflict upon ourselves.

Convincing our own hearts and minds that choosing to stay in a toxic relationship somehow equates to having control. In truth, true empowerment lies not in deceiving ourselves, but in bravely acknowledging the need for change and finding the strength to break free.

REFLECTIONS & REVELATIONS

DATE:

Journal Reflection:

- How do you recognize when you might be deceiving yourself, and what emotions typically come with that realization?
- What do you think drives someone to hide the truth from themselves, and how can self-deception affect personal growth?

Discussion Questions:

- Have you ever convinced yourself to stay in a relationship, knowing deep down it wasn't right?
- How do you know when you're lying to yourself versus making a real choice for yourself?

HE IS ALL YOURS!!

XOXO

HIS SHIT

SIS! YOU MISUNDERSTOOD

Sis, you misunderstood! You can have him, truly.
No need to feel insecure, or wonder unduly.
His time here with me, it's over and done,
I'm grateful to you, you've helped set me free, hon.

I asked God to guide me, to help me let go
Of this bad relationship— an absolute shit show.
And just like a magician, with a top hat and flair,
You appeared, abracadabra! He's now yours to bear.

Don't misunderstand my silence, it's not pain,
But joy so profound, words can't explain.
I'm absent from drama, the usual breakup scene.
I'm soaking in peace, my world-happier than ever seen.

Don't misunderstand my calm, it's not apathy.
It's the quiet celebration of newfound liberty.
So, here's to you, Sis, for the role that you played,
In orchestrating his exit, my heart is unafraid.

I'm basking in freedom, my soul is unconfined.
Thank you for being the catalyst, for easing my mind.
No hard feelings, no tears left to cry,
Just gratitude and peace, looking up at a clear, open sky.

So, Sis, you misunderstood, there's no need to fight.
He's yours, all yours, and I'm gonna be alright.

REFLECTIONS & REVELATIONS

DATE:

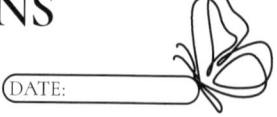

Journal Reflection:

- How does the speaker's sense of peace and freedom after the breakup challenge the typical emotions we associate with letting go? Have you ever felt similar relief in a situation that others might not understand?
- The poem expresses gratitude toward the person who 'took' the relationship. How can reframing difficult situations, like the end of a relationship, help in finding closure and inner peace?

Discussion Questions:

- Have you ever felt grateful to someone for taking a burden off your shoulders, even if they didn't realize it?
- How would you celebrate your own version of "newfound liberty" after a bad breakup?
- What's the funniest or most unexpected way someone has "helped" you get out of a relationship?

Dance to Keep from Crying!

P.S.A.

Bitch Ass Boys Grow into Bitch Ass Men. That is the message!

PICK ME
PICK ME
pick me

ADDICTED TO BEING CHOSEN

Not sure if it's the romcoms she watched as a child
Or her imaginary love stories running wild,
But in every scenario, she needed to be chosen,
Dreaming of love like a heart left unbroken.

Why is that? Is it the thrill that excites her,
Or the fear of being left out, haunting silently?
Why does she find herself addicted to being the one
Chasing approval like the setting sun?

Pick me, pick me, like a caged bird longing to be free.

Is it love that she seeks, or just the role of being loved?
Could it be the idea of being someone's first choice, undisturbed
That captivates her or, the illusion it brings?
A completeness, as if she had wings.

Can she find fulfillment within herself,
Or will she always crave the gaze of someone else?
What is it about being chosen that feels so vital?
Is she searching for love, or just a title?

Does it stem from a fear, or a desire to validate?
Is this need a mask for insecurities innate?
Addicted to being chosen, to prove she wasn't wrong,
He was the problem all along.

REFLECTIONS & REVELATIONS

DATE:

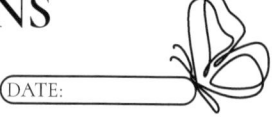

Journal Reflection:

- What do you think sparks the need to be chosen in love? Have you ever caught yourself chasing approval, and how did it make you feel?
- Is it the excitement of love or the fear of being left out that pulls you in? How do you balance your own needs with the desire for connection?

Discussion Questions:

- Do you think the need to be "chosen" comes from society, personal experiences, or a little of both?
- Have you ever chased the feeling of being someone's first choice, even when you knew it wasn't right?
- What advice would you give to someone who's addicted to the idea of being "picked" instead of finding peace within themselves?

REPAIR SHOP BLUES

Fix them, save them, nurture them—
women pour their hearts into the unending task of caring.
But have you ever stopped to consider that perhaps there is no cure,
for they never yearned salvation?

AN AFTERTHOUGHT

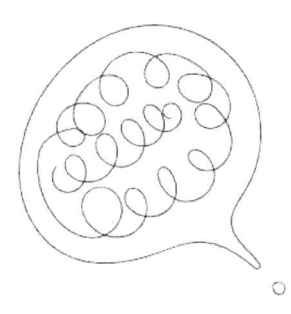

The tension between them was so thick, it could be felt like a heavy fog that had settled between their bodies. The air seemed to shimmer with the unspoken words and unexpressed emotions that hung between them. They both remained silent, locked in a fierce battle of wills, each waiting for the other to break the barrier and communicate their hidden expectations.

Time passed and the silence grew thicker, suffocating any chance of reconciliation. Was it because they were too comfortable in their frequent arguments? Too afraid to confront the deep-seated fears and vulnerabilities within themselves? Their constant conflicts had become a shield, protecting them from the difficult work of building a strong relationship.

Now, as they faced the aftermath of another fight, she couldn't help but wonder if it was all worth it. Was the temporary satisfaction of winning an argument worth losing what could have been a beautiful partnership? The answer seemed to hang in the air, elusive and unattainable, just like their ability to communicate openly and, honestly with each other.

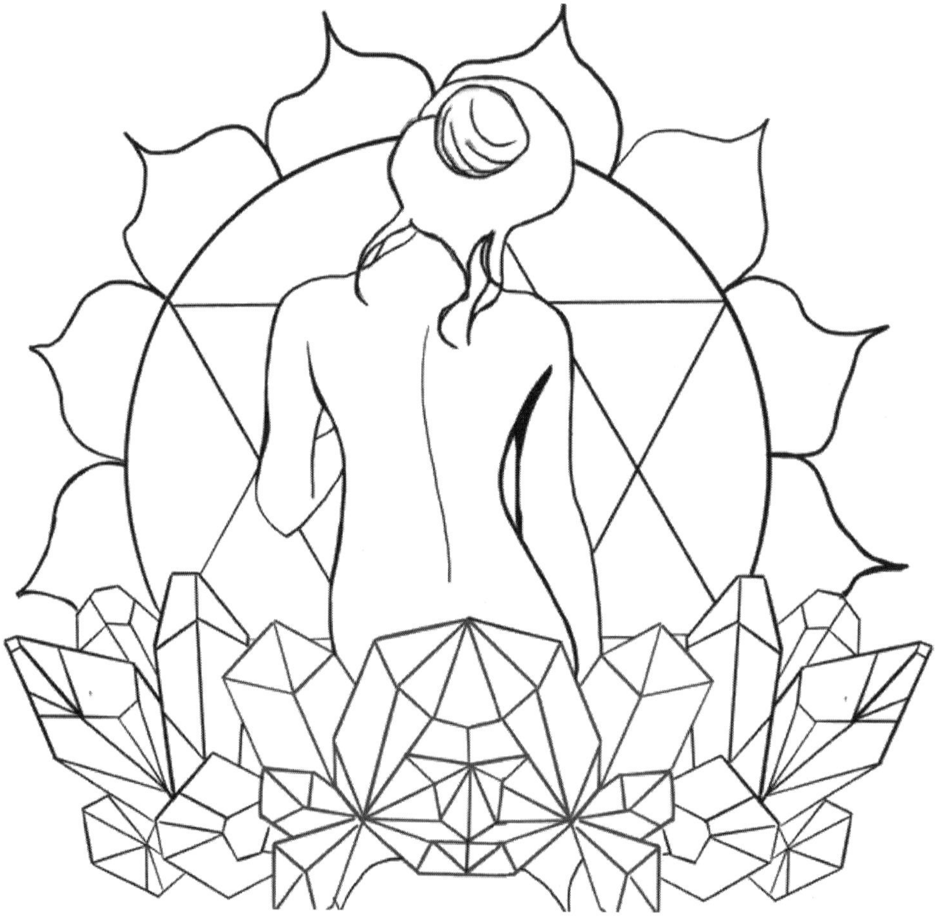

HEALING METAPHORS

Healing from a bad relationship,
Is like sifting through gravel,
Seeking hidden coins in the rubble,
Delicate as ribbons, softening sharp edges.
Comfort like marshmallows, in vulnerability.
Light as balloons, lifting your heart anew.
Gentle as cotton balls, cushioning against hurt,
Slipping into silky pajamas, warmth and security.
Yet, it's lifting a medicine ball, strength required,
Building emotional muscles, resilient and strong,
It's not a direct step-by-step process,
Sometimes, you have to restart, and that's okay.
Healing is a path, not a race,
Each step, a testament,
Now damn, go put a smile on your face.

SILENT EROSION:

HE CHEATED ON HER WITH COMPLACENCY

In the end, it wasn't the bouts of betrayal
that faded their love's flame,
But the silent erosion of ambition.
For she craved the dance of life's adventures,
While he lingered in the comfort of inertia.

Her eyes saw the world as a canvas,
awaiting radiant strokes of passion.
He remained content in the muted shades of complacency.
This love didn't perish from broken oaths,
But from a silent longing for more.
Her garden yearned for his hands to tend,
But he paid no interest for months on end,
She cried, "Awaken, dear heart, from this slumber so deep."
As her eternal waters grew still, drunk with disappointment, so steep.
Blossoms once in attention, now thrived only in the wind.

He felt he didn't have to strive anymore,
now he watched her slip away, through the unlocked door.

SABOTAGE SHENANIGANS

The mind is where self-doubt quietly dwells,
She finds her spirit caught in tangled, crippling spells.
Self-sabotage, leaves her frozen underneath,
scandalous thief in the night,
Binds her wings, keeping her from flight.

Comfort zones, though warm and cozy, become a cage,
A prison built by fear and silent rage.
She wears the mask that she chooses for others to see,
But in her eyes, she knows she has lost the essence of all life could be.

REFLECTIONS & REVELATIONS

DATE:

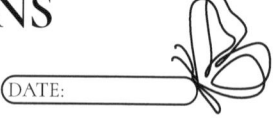

Journal Reflection:

- How do comfort zones in your life hold you back, and what fears keep you from stepping outside them?
- When have you felt like self-doubt or self-sabotage kept you from pursuing something important? How did you break free from it, or what might help you do so?
- What mask do you find yourself wearing for others, and what would it take for you to remove it and live more authentically?

Discussion Questions:

- How do you handle those moments of self-doubt or self-sabotage when they sneak in?
- Have you ever felt like you were your own worst enemy, and how did you stop the sabotage?

_____
_____
_____
_____
_____
_____
_____
_____
_____

LOOK AT YOU, BEING YOUR OWN HUSBAND

Look at you, standing tall, tools in hand,
Fixing that leaky faucet, tightening the loose stand.
You paint the walls, hammer the nails,
As if waiting for someone's help would ever prevail.
Imagine this: a man who you shared vows,
Promised forever, but where is he now?
Standing right beside you, yet you're still alone,
Bearing the weight of a house, a home.
The vows were spoken, but actions are few,
Leaving the load all up to you.
A ring on your finger, a bond in name,
But the struggles you carry hover in shame.
He's there in body, absent in care,
Leaving you stranded while he pretends unaware.
You fix the leaks, patch every damn crack,
While his empty promises leave prints on your back.
You hold your own when the night turns cold,
No arms to catch you, no hand to hold.
You are the warmth in your own embrace,
The soothing voice that keeps steady pace.
He's in the next room, yet worlds away,
And you keep it together, day by day.
Look at you, a woman of strength,
Stretching yourself beyond every length.

You mend the walls and soothe your soul,
Filling the gaps where love should be whole.
Look at you, creating your own peace,
While promises of partnership quietly cease.
There he is, a husband in name, but in truth, it's you—
The one who's been there, seeing it through.

REFLECTIONS & REVELATIONS

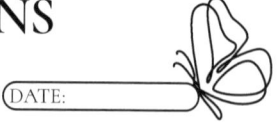

DATE:

Journal Reflection:

- How does the poem make you reflect on the balance of effort in your own relationships? Have you ever felt like you were carrying the weight alone?
- What emotions come up when thinking about unfulfilled promises or expectations? How do you handle the gap between words and actions in your own life?

Discussion Questions:

- How do you think society's expectations of partnership play into the idea of 'fixing things yourself'?
- Do you feel pressure to be independent, even when in a relationship?

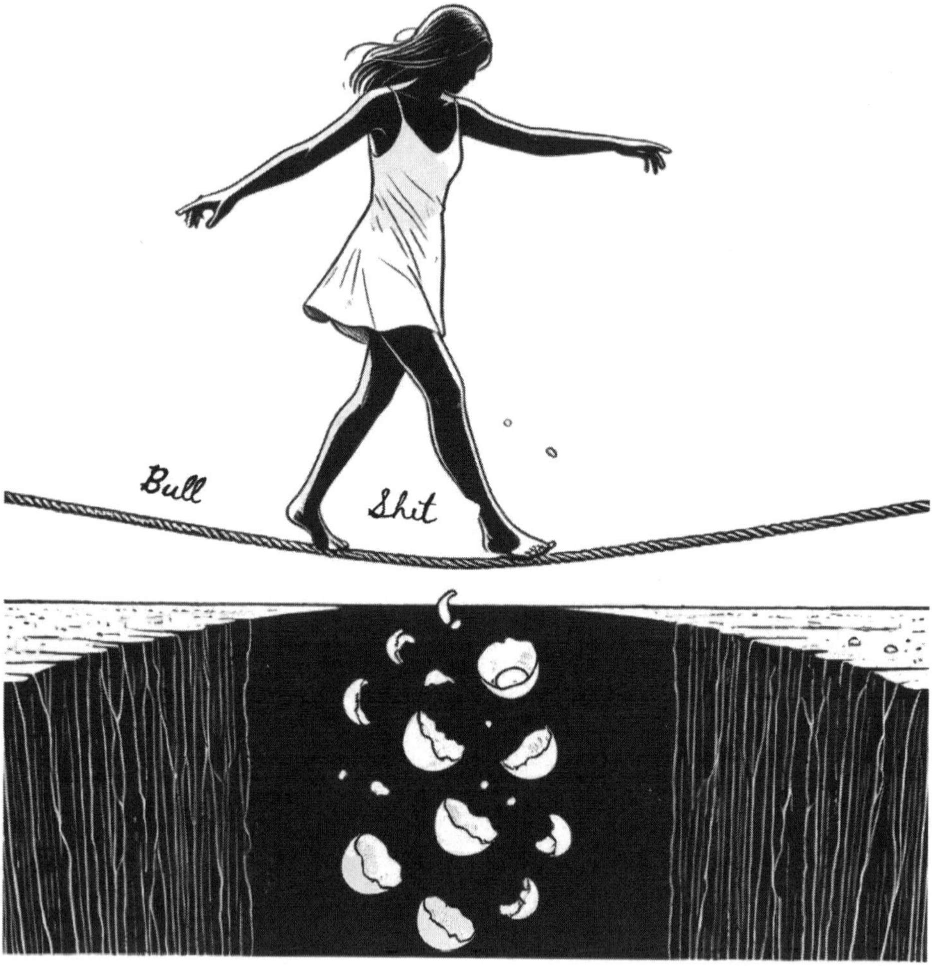
Bull
Shit

TIGHT ROPES AND EGGSHELLS

WARNING - MENTION OF DOMESTIC VIOLENCE

Her desire to please him disgusts her now, as she looks back. Her posture had grown timid, her voice rising a few octaves, almost childlike when she spoke to him, always gauging the mood he was in. She held conversations rarely, meeting his eyes less and less as the days drew on, hiding from necessary confrontations to avoid awakening the beast of his temper.

She had once navigated life with the bold strides of someone who knew where they were going, unafraid of challenges. But that was before she met him. He swept into her life with declarations that dazzled, painting a future so vivid it blinded her to the present. As the days passed, the promises dimmed, replaced by the grays of a reality she hadn't agreed to.

At first, his mood swings seemed like mere quirks, a small price for the whirlwind of romance. But as his darker moods became more frequent, she found herself walking a tightrope, balancing above a chasm that threatened to swallow her whole. Her words became lighter, like eggshells scattered on the path of their daily existence, brittle and ready to crack under the slightest misstep.

She learned to retreat, to make herself smaller, less noticeable. Her reflections in the mirror began to frighten her as if her true self was fading away, leaving behind a shadow too afraid to speak up, to exist. She hid from confrontations, big and small, tiptoeing around his temper to keep the peace, to keep the beast at bay. She knew she should leave, but her pride sought no reprieve.

Now, on no particular Wednesday, she stands looking over her body. No more to be hidden, no more to endure Departed at noon, silenced too soon.

THE COLORS OF A MOCKERY

Peek in the gallery of my heart, where a circus unfolds,
With acts of stupidity and stories unfold.

Red, the color of the clown's nose, so bright,
Masking tears that fall, out of sight, out of light.

Oh, the red flags waved—a big top's grand array,
"I love you too quickly," and *"Let's run away."*
With each jest and tumble, I played the fool,
Laughing on the outside, breaking every rule.

Green was the grass where the circus tents stood,
Where we cast aside caution, as we knew we would.
"It'll be different this time," we'd cheer in refrain,
Spinning through acts that bordered on the insane.

Black were the curtains, behind which I'd hide,
From the audience's gaze, where our true selves reside.
A backstage of sorrow, where clowns go to weep,
Far from the laughter, in shadows deep.

Yet, here in the end, as the big top comes down,
The colors are mellowing, from bright to brown.
No more charades, clown suit retired,
Embracing a calm, I've so long desired.

HER LIGHT, HIS ENVY

Instead of growing with her, he stands aloof.
Quietly thriving in her mishaps, his secret ruse.
False words of support, a deceitful guise,
His envy simmering, masked in lies.
Jealous of her accomplishments, he watches in spite.
Her successes a reflection, exposing his plight.
In obscurity, he lingers, his true self exposed,
Her light reveals his envy, a burden unopposed.

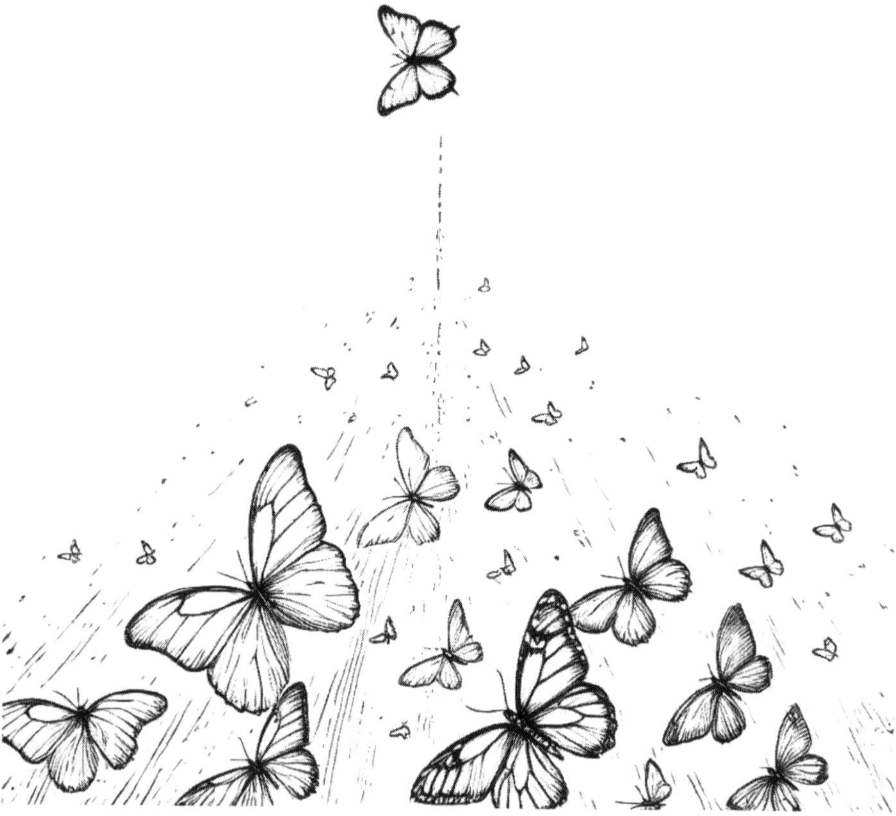

EMBARRASSED ISOLATION

Numerous warnings, friends' distant calls.
Alone she sits, in this cold embrace,
A heart confined, an empty space.

They saw the signs, the red flags raised,
Their voices clear, their concern unfazed.
Yet here she lingers in this silent fight,
Embarrassed, lost, in the dead of night.

Their words of wisdom, now echoes past,
She clung to love, though it couldn't last.
Isolation swallows her whole, chilling and proud,
In this dark room, silence speaks loud.

Fear grips tight, of what they'll say,
The dreaded "We told you so" harpooned her way.
Ashamed to face the truth she spurned, they were right
Now, in solitude, she plans her exit without a fight.
Their calls have faded, no more to plead,
They know the truth: and she must now heed.

REFLECTIONS & REVELATIONS

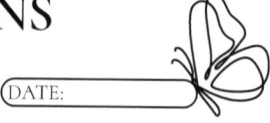

DATE:

Journal Reflection:

- How does ignoring others' warnings affect your sense of self in relationships?
- What does isolation teach you about the reality of a relationship?

Discussion Questions:

- Have you ever stayed in a bad relationship out of embarrassment, worrying what people would say?
- What advice would you give someone who feels too ashamed to leave but knows they need to?
- How do you find the strength to reach out to friends after isolating yourself in a toxic situation?

_____
_____
_____
_____
_____
_____
_____
_____
_____
_____

NOTES

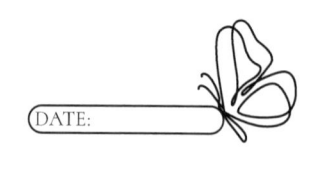

DATE:

NOTES

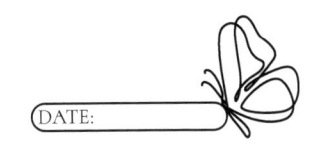

DATE:

NOTES

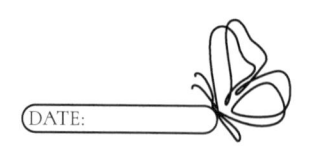

DATE:

NOTES

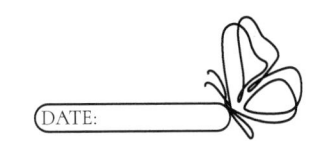

DATE:

NOTES

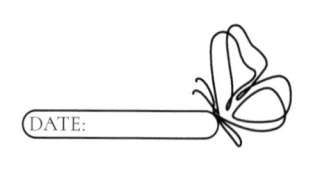

DATE:

NOTES

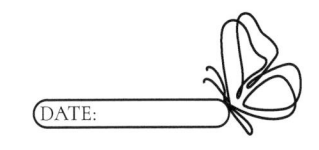

DATE:

PIECES TO PEACE

PIECES   DOING THE WORK   PEACE

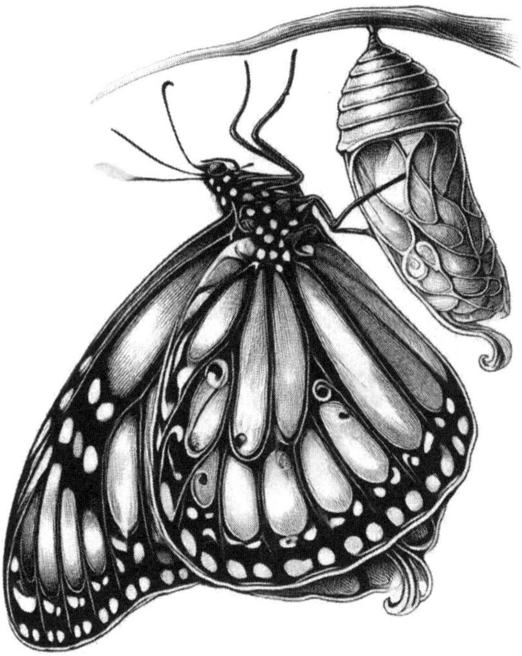

PIECES TO PEACE

To heal a wound, you must cleanse it, stop touching it—
this truth applies not just to the flesh, but to the heart as well.
Love, in its most tender form, requires the bravery to step back,
to let the air of solitude mend what was torn.
Every touch, though meant with love,
can sometimes reopen the very scars we wish to heal.

It's in the quiet absence, the gentle space between,
where healing brews its subtle magic.
We must learn to love from a distance,
to send our affections in whispers, not in waves.

Time, the silent healer,
works best when we're not watching, not pressing.
So, let the wound breathe, let the heart plead, and in that yearning,
may it find its way back to whole, back to love.

*No longer in pieces, just now at **PEACE**.*

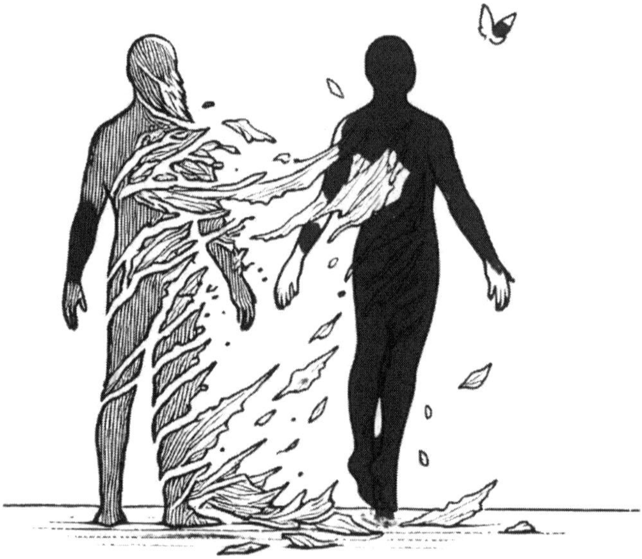

SHEDDING IS HEALING

Shedding is necessary for healing, but it's not easy. It's like a butterfly breaking free from its cocoon or a snake shedding its old skin - it's painful and uncomfortable. She knows she needs to let go of the past and move on, but part of her wants to hold onto her pain and use it as a shield against the world.

But staying in this mess won't make her stronger. It's time for her to heal, even if it means losing some friends in the process. Each time she looks in the mirror, she sees a new piece of herself emerging, and it both excites and scares her. Can she really leave behind her fears, traumas, and negative thoughts? Can she embrace self-love and courage?

She'll have to let go of toxic relationships and beliefs that have held her back for so long. It won't be easy, but she knows the freedom and strength that will come with it will be worth it. Healing is a journey, one that will reveal her true self and bring her closer to who she is meant to be. It's scary, but she's ready to take that first step towards letting go and embracing growth.

GRACE

Hey there!

Give yourself grace.
Forgive yourself for past decisions.
You haven't lived this exact life before;
you chose based on what you believed was best at the time.

As you grow wiser, don't use that wisdom to ridicule your past choices. They were the stepping stones that brought you to your current place of growth and understanding.

Forgiveness starts with taking accountability and knowing it begins within. Embrace your journey with compassion.

Let your past guide you, not define you. However, if you find yourself making the same bad decisions over and over, consciously deciding to do things you know are unwise, then that's on you. Own your choices and strive to do better.

Note: *If you find yourself in a never-ending cycle of making questionable decisions, it might be a good time to call that therapist!*

REFLECTIONS & REVELATIONS

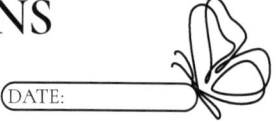

DATE:

Journal Reflection:

- Make a list of past decisions in relationships you're holding onto. How can you start forgiving yourself for them?
- Think of a time when you gave yourself grace in a relationship. How did it help you move forward?

Discussion Questions:

- How do you practice giving yourself grace in relationships, especially after making mistakes?
- What role does self-forgiveness play in moving forward from past decisions in relationships?
- When is it important to seek outside help, like therapy, to break harmful patterns in relationships?

FORGIVE AND FORGET

Forgive and forget, they chant like a spell,
Words that beg for peace, a softening of hell.
A mantra to quiet the abuse of the heart,
A pledge to erase, to grant a fresh start.
But memories linger, refusing to stay at a distance,
Declining to fade, intrusive in their persistence.

Damn! Those "forgotten" memories, they never really rest.
They climb on my back in the dead of the night,
Tugging at my hair, gripping me tight.
Whispering tales of the times I tried to erase,
Asking for stories, a smile on their face.
Can one truly forget the pain once it's sewn?
Do we just bury it, cold and alone?
Yet in the chant, there lies a gentle call,
To rise above grievances, to let grudges fall.

**Ugh! No one told me that forgiveness isn't merely words we declare,
It's a journey, so thick, a kind of repair.**
We must sit with our pain, not brush it aside,
Face our upheavals within, with eyes open wide.
**I wish I knew that there was much more than saying the words,
I Forgive You!**
Maybe then, I wouldn't have resented you,
It's too late now to go back you see, for our expiration is long overdue.

I'VE LEARNED, I'VE LEARNED

The Art of Unlearning

I've learned that love should not be a field of mines.
I've learned that silence can scream that quiet might bleed,
And that neglect, dressed as freedom, is a treacherous seed.

I've learned, I've learned, from nights too long,
That the ring that never finds its place on a hand,
Is a sign, not of love, but of unwanted plans.

I've learned that whispered commitments, brittle and thin,
Are not just oversights, but deeper sins.
And words that mock, not mend, reveal
A heart not joined in joy, but concealed in shields.

I've learned, I've learned, from excuses that wane,
That avoidance of truth is the real ball and chain.

Big, Big Fact: Avoiding brief exchanges crafts, a kaleidoscope of missed connections, leaving us navigating a life riddled with dysfunction. Say what the fuck you feel and don't sit in that mess day after day, year after year.

Write this down: Avoidance leads to dysfunction.

REFLECTIONS & REVELATIONS

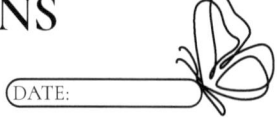

DATE:

Journal Reflection:

- What truths have you avoided confronting, and how has that avoidance acted as a "ball and chain" in your life?
- What would change if you embraced the idea of saying exactly how you feel, rather than sitting in unspoken frustrations?

Discussion Questions:

- What's one of the biggest lessons you've had to "unlearn" in relationships?
- How do you deal with those "silent screams" in relationships where things feel off, but no one is saying anything?
- What's your advice for avoiding that "dysfunction" that comes from avoiding tough conversations?

_____
_____
_____
_____
_____
_____
_____
_____
_____
_____

THE COST OF QUIET ACCEPTANCE

Lessons learned from my mother's silence,
Her quiet ways, a guide misunderstood.
She taught me calm, a subtle compliance,
Acceptance of far less than I ever should.

Lessons learned from my mother's silence,
Each unspoken grievance behind her mask she bore.
Her endurance mistaken for resilience,
Enduring what should be abhorred.

Lessons learned from my mother's silence,
Echoes of her voiceless fears resonate.
Mimicking her quiet compliance,
Learning to embrace a similar fate.
Lessons learned from my mother's silence,
Acceptance taught without a fight.
Now I see, through a clearer lens,
Silence was surrender, masked as right.

SINS OF HER FATHER

Is she paying for the sins of her father,
As the fragments of his choices linger?
Her father was no easy love for her mother.
Endless it was, his presence, an energy draining figure.

Is she paying for the sins of her father,
Where truth was warped in the light of his ways?
He never really lied,
Blatant in his betrayals, unmasked in his plays.

Is she paying for the sins of her father,
As her mother's memories softly shift?
Painting past pains with a gentler brush,
Turning harsh truths into myths.

Is she paying for the sins of her father,
In the love that she seeks, in the love that she gives?
Learning from a map drawn by flawed hands,
Finding herself where she once prayed, she'd never live.

DILUTED ESSENCE

A woman once stood fierce and tall,
Unafraid to sever ties, she'd rise from each fall.
Rebuilding herself, shielding from deep within,
Before letting anyone beneath her skin.
Sadly, one day, a hummingbird flew through her window.
Landed softly, with a gentle glow.
A song only her heart could hear.
Its melody, sweet, whispering hope near.

But soon it vanished, held captive by chains unseen,
Its freedom stolen, like a faded dream.
Years passed, and the hummingbird returned,
No longer with sweet songs it once had churned.
It transformed into a mockingbird, mocking glee,
Winding its way into her soul, so free.
Under the guise of husband, a serpent he'd become.
Riding her coattails, masking insecurity's scum.

This mockingbird, a puppeteer pulling strings,
Controlled her world, every ounce, every thing.
No longer singing, just chipping away,
Silently eroding her essence each day.
Worn by the dance of staying or leaving,
She chose to relinquish her strength, for peace seeming.
Becoming his mouthpiece to justify his wrongs,
A puppet, manipulated, her self-respect now gone.

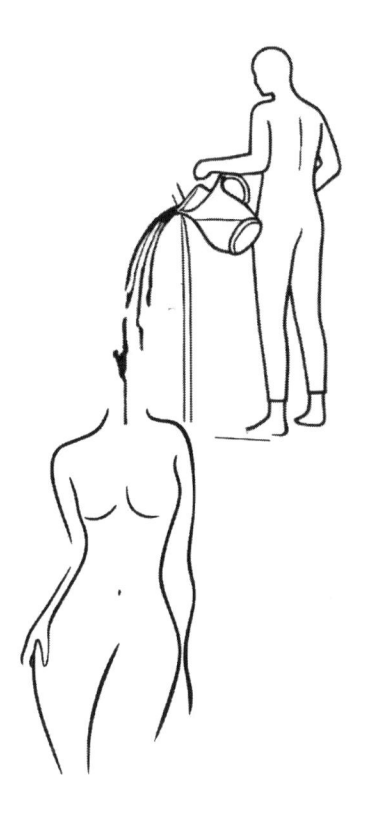

His help, a guise not of love but obligation,
Leaving her bound, tethered to his dictation.
She had strived so hard, yet stood as a fool,
Her essence, once bright, now dried as drool.
A reflection of her former self, trapped,
In the dance with a serpent, forever snapped.
Her vibrant spirit by deceit diluted.
Her song now a whisper, her light convoluted.
She looked into her mirror and couldn't see.
She hid in her closet thinking,
whatever happened to being Masterfully ME?

REFLECTIONS & REVELATIONS

DATE:

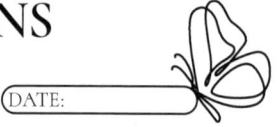

Journal Reflection:

- How do you relate to the woman's journey of rebuilding herself after setbacks, and what has helped you rise after your own falls?
- When have you felt the need to shield yourself from others, and what would it take for you to let someone beneath your guard again?

Discussion Questions:

- Have you ever felt like you lost your true self in a relationship, and how did you find your way back?
- How do you keep your "essence" intact when someone is trying to chip away at it?
- What's your biggest lesson from a relationship where you felt like you gave up too much of who you are?

_____

_____

_____

_____

_____

_____

_____

_____

_____

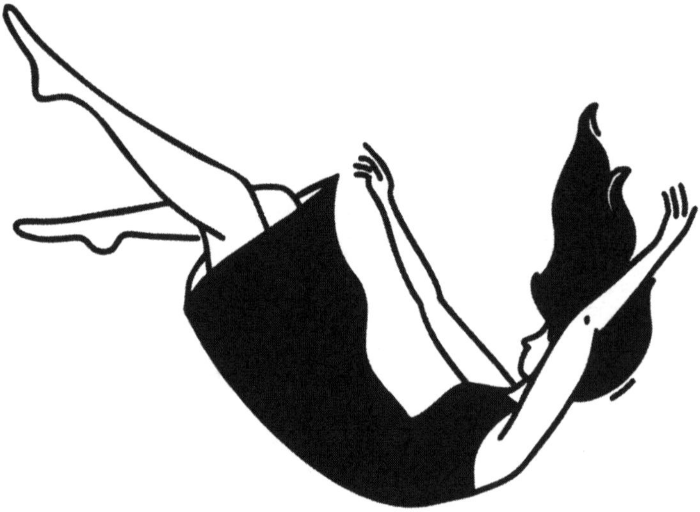

FREEFALL - NO ANCHOR

She stood at the edge, peeking into her heart, dreams dissolving into the harsh light of understanding. With a heart full and hopeful, she had leapt fearlessly, embracing the possibility of a love that could transcend her ordinary.

She now realized that some loves, no matter how profound, were never meant to anchor us. Yet, now as she fell, the reality of her solitude became painfully clear. The hardest part of falling was not the impact of the landing, but the sudden, sharp awareness that no one would be there to catch her. Each moment in freefall stripped away layers of her naive expectations, revealing the stark truth, devoid of fabrication

Love, in its most authentic form, teaches about resilience more than companionship. And as she gathered herself from the emotional debris, she found strength in her own presence, her own solidity.

No longer waiting to be caught, she resolved to rise again.
Empowered by the knowledge that she was her own best friend.

In the quiet with her favorite pillow,
she whispered a newfound creed:
*I am the architect of my joy, the anchor for my soul,
ready to take the lead.*

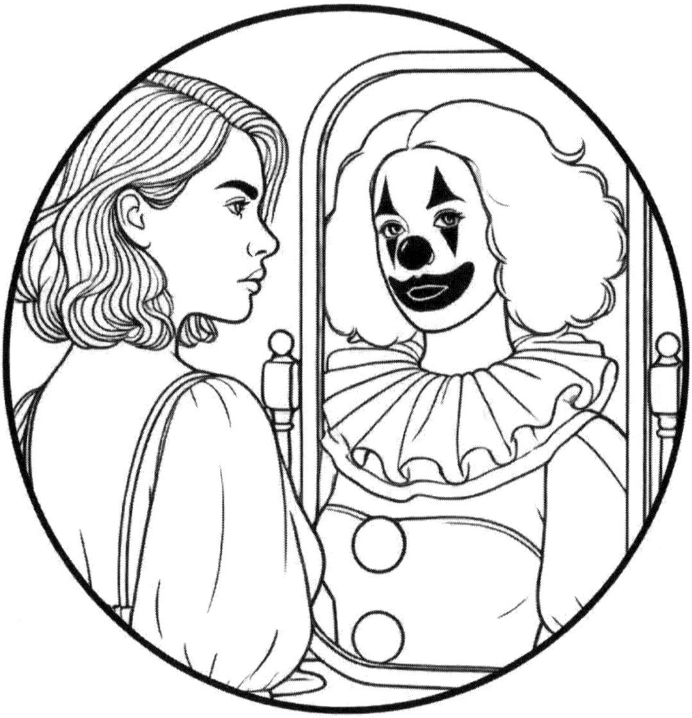

AM I THE DRAMA?

Am I the drama, the chorus whispers, am I the scene?
I saw the red flags, yet I chose to ignore them.
So, what does that say about me?

Each choice, a reflection in the mirror of my making.
I had to grab the lens, turn it to selfie mode,
No longer focusing on you, but now glaring at me,
A scrutiny sharp, an image I was not trying to see.

Am I the drama, reality mocks, am I the play?
In the theater of my own design, I set the stage,
Crafting curtains of silence, walls woven with denial.
I leave, I stay, nothing is ever final.

Every act, a step on the stage, lines laced, my confession.
Every night, I take a bow, retreat, wallow in my vexation.
Are these flags not of my own planting,
Red as the roses in a tragic romance?
I painted the scenery; I called the cues. Dang!
What the hell am I supposed to do?

Am I the drama, the whisper returns, am I the spectacle?
In turning the lens, I see not just a face but outlined scars,
A tale where I am both playwright and star. So, am I the drama?
Perhaps just human, I see the role I play, no need to intervene,
Learning, through messy lines and repeated scenes,
That in every act, there is a chance to rewrite the script,
so much still to be seen.

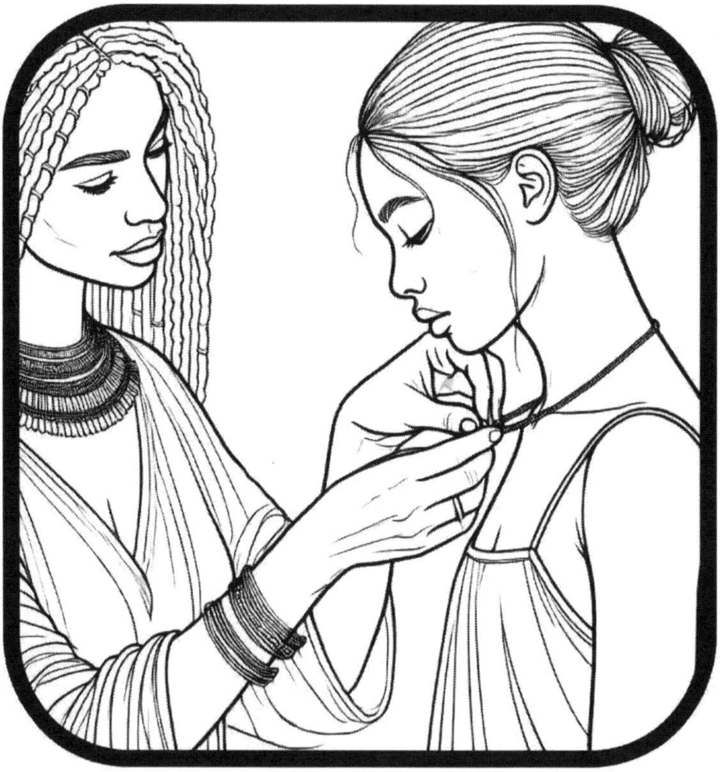

MOTHER'S CHAINS

Right down the road, a tale unfolds,
Of a daughter's journey, yet untold.
Her mother, once, with fearful eyes,
Stayed in a bond, where love was disguised.
A bad relationship, blanketed in shame,
For the whispers of the neighborhood's name.
Separate bedrooms, affection denied,
A quiet misery, they both tried to hide.

Now the daughter, as years unfold,
Finds herself trapped, her spirit sold.
Enduring all that she once gazed upon,
Praying for strength, a chance to move on.

She cares not for others, their judgments untold,
Breaking free from the mold they behold.
An invisible barrier holds her tight,
Accepting mere crumbs, as signs of love's light.
Does she desire too much, she questions within,
Bound by the doubts that twist and spin.
Is this her fate, the place she should be?
Now, her children are watching,
what do they see?

REFLECTIONS & REVELATIONS

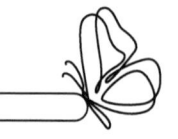

DATE:

Journal Reflection:

- Do you think we unconsciously repeat the relationship patterns we see growing up?
- How do you break free from the emotional "chains" passed down through generations?
- What advice would you give to someone who feels trapped in a situation similar to what they witnessed as a child?

Discussion Questions:

- Have you ever made a conscious decision to break a cycle in your family, and how did you go about it?
- What does "true love" look like to you, especially when compared to unhealthy versions of love you might have seen?
- How do you find the courage to choose a different path for yourself and future generations?

BEYOND FEAR AND MUCK

The most significant breakthrough can't happen simply because of fear and a willingness to settle in the muck.

True progress demands more than just enduring discomfort—it requires a proactive leap toward transformation, paired with a touch of liberosis, the freeing desire to care less about the vines that hold us back.

It's about using fear as a signal to act, not an excuse to stagnate, while letting go of the weight of unnecessary worries.

Refusing to settle in the muck means seeking clarity and striving for growth, liberating oneself from the shadows of doubt, even when the path is obscured.

Breakthroughs are built on the foundation of action and the gentle release of our grip on control, not the resignation to circumstances..

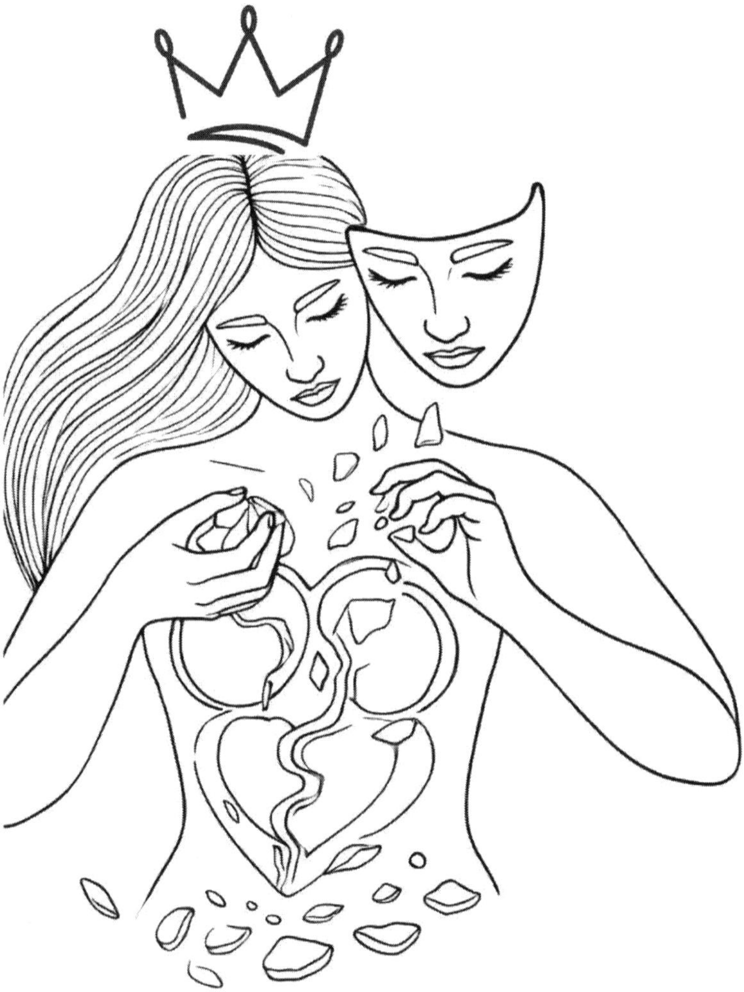

SOUL ARCHITECT

Now, in the stillness of my existence,
I find myself amidst the remnants of a once vibrant spirit.

Where laughter and dreams once merged,
There now lingers a haunting emptiness.
The void keeps me in a chokehold,
Where memories used to bloom like wildflowers in the sun.
With tender hands and blueprints unrolled wide,
I sketch the outlines of a soul redesigned.

Foundation laid with stones of past regret,
Mortared by forgiveness, I won't forget
The lessons etched in every broken beam—
From rubble rise, transform each shattered dream.

The framework rises, timber bent with care,
Each beam a choice, each nail a simple prayer.
Windows wide to let the morning in,
Glass reflects what lies within.

The roof, a canopy of newfound hope,
Shelters peace, a scope wide as my heart can hope,
Of starry skies that assure dark will fade,
Underneath, my quietude is laid.
Inside, I paint with colors bold and bright,

Shades of a happy life shimmer in the light.
Textures soft as kindness, spread each wall,
A canvas broad, life's mural to install.

Gardens bloom from seeds of gentle deeds,
Paths emerge where my spirit leads.
Flowers named for every cherished friend,
Roots that ground, branches that ascend.

Now I step back, a home rebuilt anew,
Harmony in every stone and view.
Architect of soul, I hold the key,
To chambers vast as possibility.

In the art of living, I architect.
A dwelling made with patience, crafted slow,
In its halls, my truest self I know.

Inside, I paint with colors bold and bright,
Shades of a happy life shimmer in the light.
Textures soft as kindness, spread each wall,
A canvas broad, life's mural to install.

Gardens bloom from seeds of gentle deeds,
Paths emerge where my spirit leads.
Flowers named for every cherished friend,
Roots that ground, branches that ascend.

Now I step back, a home rebuilt anew,
Harmony in every stone and view.
Architect of soul, I hold the key,
To chambers vast as possibility.

In the art of living, I architect.
A dwelling made with patience, crafted slow,
In its halls, my truest self I know.

REFLECTIONS & REVELATIONS

DATE:

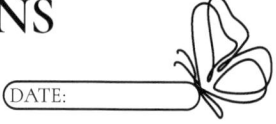

Journal Reflection:

- What would your "soul blueprint" look like if you could design it for your happiest self?
- What does isolation teach you about the reality of a relationship?

Discussion Questions:

- Have you ever felt like you had to "rebuild" yourself after a major emotional setback?
- How do you create a solid foundation for your emotional well-being after going through a tough time?

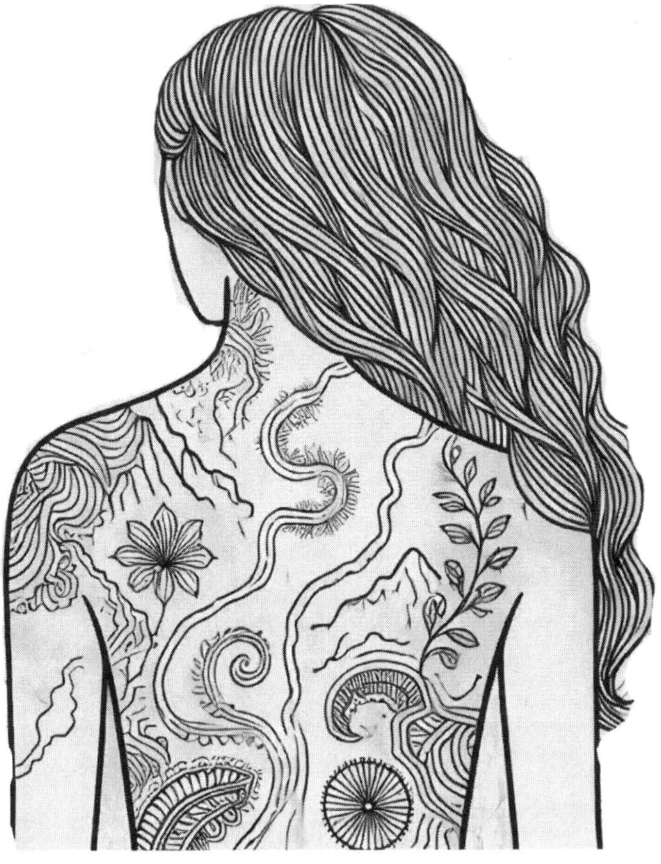

DON'T RUN!
LET THE SCARS GUIDE YOU

Making destiny moves is challenging when guided by historical pain. Our past actions and regrets, if left unaddressed, keep us stagnant. To move forward, one must sit with these memories, understanding them not as reminders of pain, but as beautiful scars.

These scars are testimonies, not to the pain endured, but to the battles fought and overcome. They should not serve as anchors but as milestones of perseverance.

Each scar is a story of survival, a badge of courage. Recognizing them as such transforms them from burdens into symbols of strength. This shift in perception is essential for growth and forward movement.

Only by accepting and embracing these scars can we truly make destiny moves. They are not just marks of past pains but beacons of future triumphs.

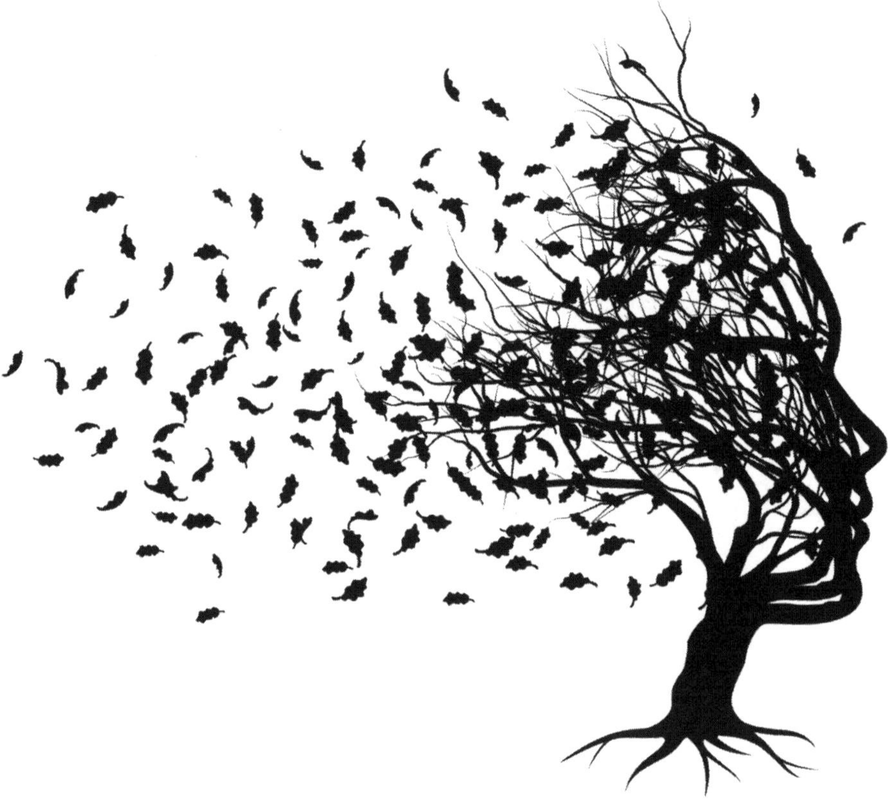

ILLUSION VS DELUSION

As we go through life there is so much to discern,
A mirage in the desert, a dream in the night,
A conniving soul just out of sight.
Yet delusion creeps in with a sinister grin,
A darkened specter that dwells deep within.
It cloaks the mind with deceptive grace,
A falsehood that time struggles to erase.
We chase illusions, with hearts full of fire,
Dreaming of futures, climbing ever higher.
But delusion's grip can twist and bend,
Turning dreams into nightmares, without end.
So, tread with care, in the twilight's gleam,
Between the worlds of reality and dream.
Embrace the illusions that make you whole,
But beware the delusions that can steal your soul.

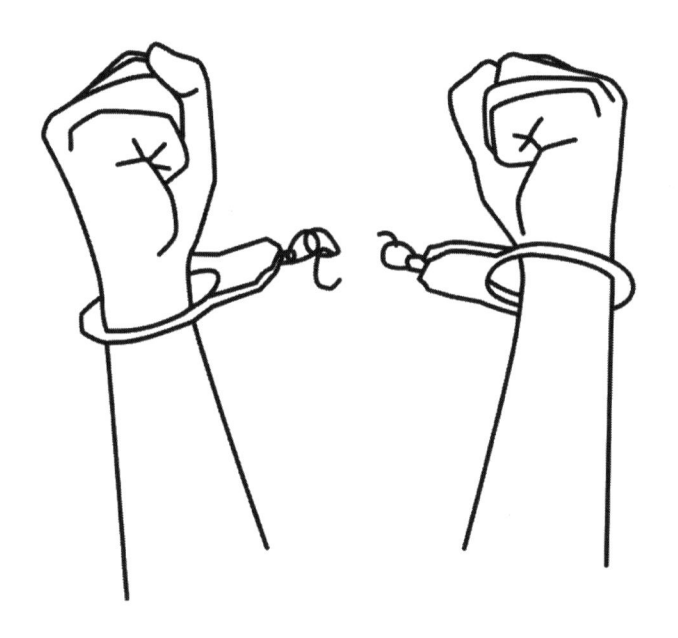

THE SHACKLES OF LOYALTY

Loyalty, a virtue both noble and rare, often binds us in chains where wisdom would dare to flee. It is a gilded wrought prison, daring and, confining that holds us captive long after the warning signs appear.

True loyalty does not mean enduring harm or turning a blind eye to deceit; it means knowing when to hold on and when to let go for the betterment of oneself and others.

There comes a time when our devotion must not be to people or past promises but to the pursuit of our own well-being and truth.

Recognizing this is not a betrayal but rather an act of courage and self-preservation, a necessary step to break free from the shackles of misguided fidelity and step into the light of self-worth and logical decision-making.

REFLECTIONS & REVELATIONS

DATE:

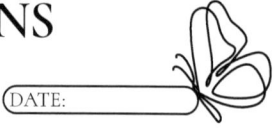

Journal Reflection:

- What's a moment when you realized that staying loyal was doing more harm than good, and how did you find the courage to break free?
- In what ways has loyalty felt like a "gilded prison" in your life, and how did you eventually break free from it, if at all?

Discussion Questions:

- Have you ever stayed loyal to someone or something, even when you knew it was no longer healthy for you?
- How do you balance loyalty to others with loyalty to yourself?

_____
_____
_____
_____
_____
_____
_____
_____
_____
_____
_____

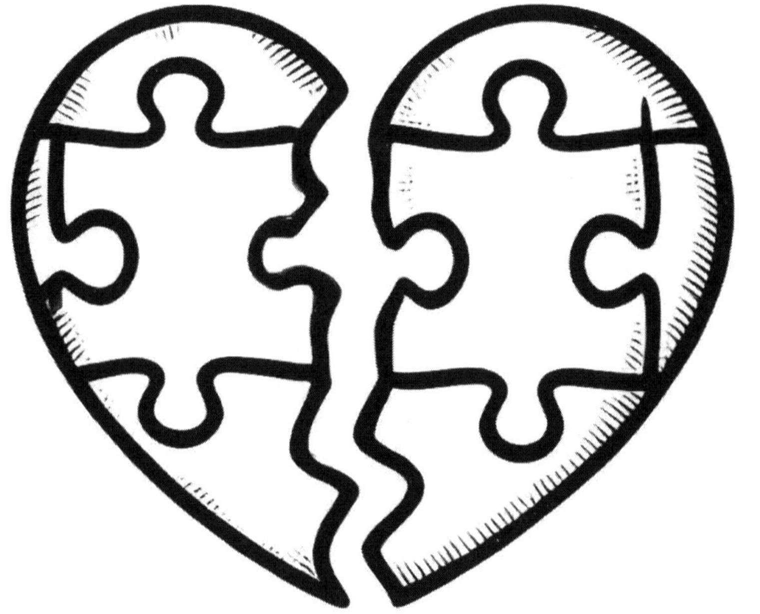

WHEN HEARTS DON'T ALIGN

I did not listen; I did not see.
Blinded by love, only you were key.
Again and again, your style of love was a clue.
Our bodies connected, but never to glue.

Over and over, you ravaged my insides,
Yet I, in my silence, ignored the wise.
My heart chose you in a reckless sprint,
Forgetting that love needs a mutual hint.

Sorry am I, for the resent that grew,
For blaming the heart that only knew you.
It was my own doing, my own silent plea,
For a love unreturned, a love not meant to be.

You never chose me, the truth I ignored,
In love's harsh lesson, my heart was floored.
Not all can be mended, not all can be right,
I learned too late, as you vanished from sight.

Let me be brave, for us both: it's time
To gather our moments, while still in our prime. BYE!

He was a beautiful terror hidden in plain sight.
Don't Blink!

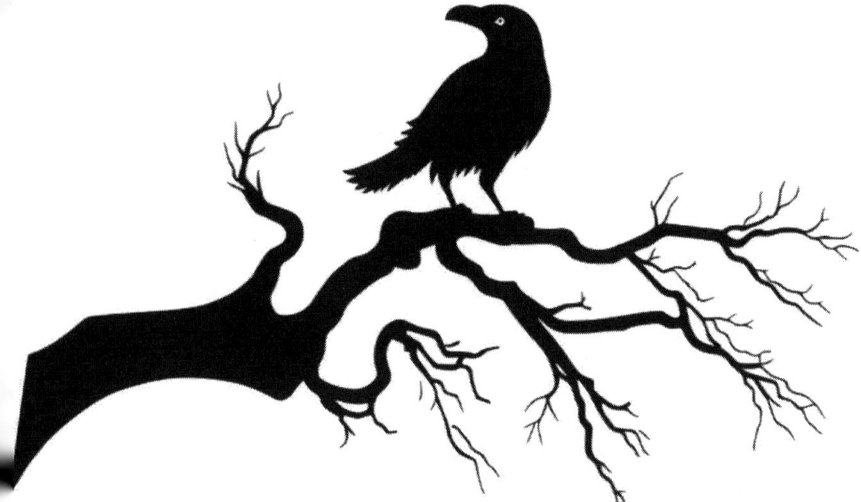

GRIEF: THE UNINVITED GUEST

Some mornings burst bright, my heart a canvas wide,
colors spilling, eager for the world's embrace.
But there are days that grief's crow comes closer still,
its weight a whisper on the edge of my existence.
Grief perches at my bedside, steps onto my chest,
its sharp talons digging into my skin as it stares
down at me with beady black eyes.
Its feathers are as dark as the depths of my despair,
casting a shadow over me in the dim morning light.
With its beak, it tears at the sheets that cover me,
a relentless reminder of my pain and loss.

It hops along the arteries of my heart,
playing hopscotch with sharp stones of memory,
each leap a stinging imprint,
each square a flashback, vivid and wrenching.

Grief, the uninvited guest with persistent grip,
reminds me of loves lost and times past.
It drenches me with rivers long damned,
flooding plains with tears unspent and words unsaid.
This time, as the crow and I sit in the quiet, its soft feathers
gently consoling me today,
I catch glimmers of a silver lining, thin and fleeting—
a reminder that to feel such depths of sorrow is
but the offset of having loved so deeply.

**It took time to see that grief and love, closely knit,
Demand each other's presence, one the result of the other,
inseparable, intertwined.**

REFLECTIONS & REVELATIONS

DATE:

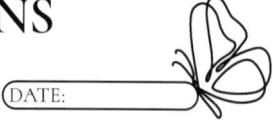

Journal Reflection:

- If grief were an animal for you, what would it be? How would you describe your own version of 'grief the crow'?
- How has your understanding of the connection between grief and love evolved, and how do you find comfort in knowing they are intertwined?

Discussion Questions:

- Have you ever had a moment when grief surprised you, like the crow in the poem? How do you usually handle unexpected feelings of sadness?
- The poem talks about finding a 'silver lining' in grief. What's something positive you've learned or experienced after going through a tough time?

LOSS: WORLD OFF ITS AXIS

World off its axis, my constant gone.
I whisper to the stars, hoping they'll convey
My voice to where you dance, beyond the moon's throng.

World off its axis, my constant gone.
Each day unfolds, heavy without your guiding sun.
Exhausted by sadness, the door slammed shut,
Echoing in my heart, where your laughter once spun.
Sometimes I wish I could pry that door.
Not to change the past, but to see your eyes once more.

World off its axis, my constant gone.
I'd breathe in your strength, let it soothe my core.
But here in the shadows, where light fears to tread,
The world turned dark; my heart turned to stone.
Unleashing my pain like splinters sharp and dread,
World off its axis, my constant gone.
Why don't you visit me in my dreams?
Is there no passage back from heavenly streams?
In the stillness, my soul suffocates, emits silent screams,
World off its axis, my constant gone.

In another world, across timeless seams,
Will you recognize me, will our bond be known?
For now, I gaze at the stars, catching their gleams.
World off its axis, my constant gone.
And though tears may blur my earthly sight,
Your essence guides me, a beacon of light.

NOTHING FOR YOU, EVERYTHING FOR ME

I tried to forgive, but these ugly reflections, won't break.
I tried to forget, but the memories lie awake.
Nothing for you resides within me anymore,
A quiet abyss, a lifeless bore.
It's empty here now, a chilling feat,
A space where love used to be.

I know you feel it too, a hollowed jest,
In the ruins of what we once professed.
The attempts at pardon, they fall through,
A haunting reminder, a shade untrue.
The effort to erase, merely a scar,
A reminder of how far we are.

No warmth left, no flicker of flame,
Just shadows of us, neither to blame.
An emptiness that speaks volumes, unspoken,
A bond once unbreakable, now broken.
So, in this void, we stand apart
With nothing but memories that dart.
Forgiveness sought, but not found.
In this silence, a profound sound.
I tried, oh how I tried, to mend what's torn,
But in the trying only more is worn.
Nothing for you, everything for me.
In this nothingness, we're finally free.

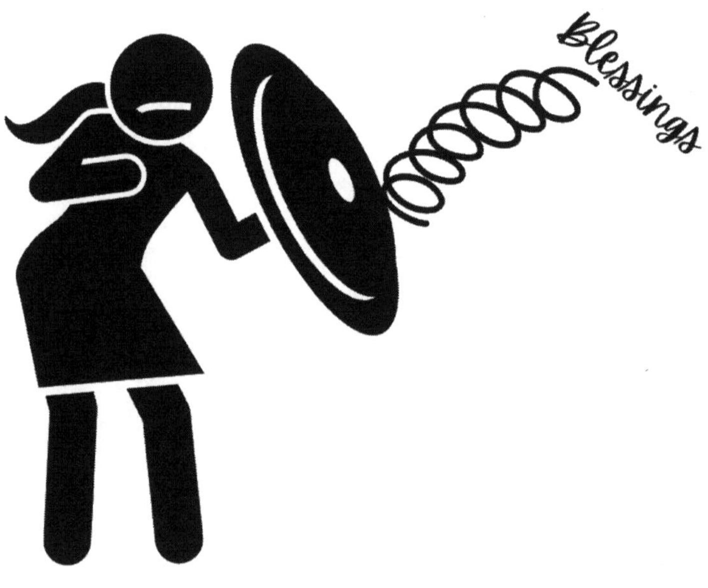
Blessings

BLOCKED BLESSINGS

Longing.
She ached to be seen and loved,
Patiently awaiting the arrival of a soul who would cherish her.
But as the seasons passed, she discovered a bitter truth—
She had wasted precious years waiting for someone, for him.
Yet simultaneously, she was blocking her
own blessings with many of her actions.
In that moment of clarity,
she realized the greatest love story
Lies not in the one who failed to see her,
But in the strength, she found to let go
and embrace her true self flaws and all.

REFLECTIONS & REVELATIONS

DATE:

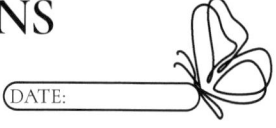

Journal Reflection:

- What actions or behaviors have you noticed in yourself that may have held you back from receiving the blessings you deserve?
- What does embracing your true self, 'flaws and all,' look like for you, and how has it impacted your life or relationships?

Discussion Questions:

- Have you ever felt like you were waiting for someone else to validate you, only to realize that self-love was what you needed all along?
- How can our own actions sometimes block the blessings or happiness we're seeking? Have you ever had a moment of clarity like this?

_____
_____
_____
_____
_____
_____
_____
_____
_____
_____

HEALINGS BEGINS WITH US

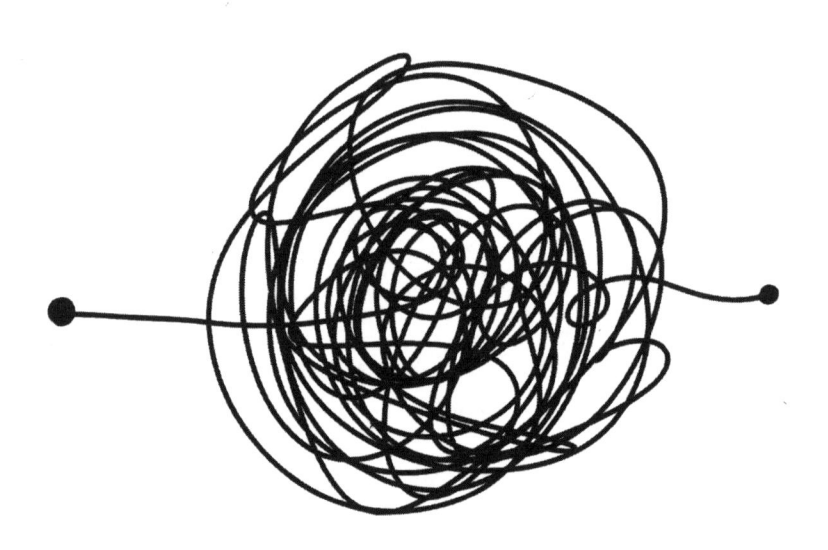

STIRRING THE POT

Honestly, some days I just wanted to cause damage
To those who hurt me, leave them in ravage.
It's a part of healing, these feelings so raw,
Acknowledging pain, the wounds that I saw.

People have feelings, it's natural, it's real,
To want retribution, to make them feel.
But in stirring the pot, I find my release,
A step in my journey towards inner peace.

The anger, the hurt, it bubbles inside,
A tornado of emotions, impossible to hide.
Yet in this misery, I begin to see,
The path to healing starts within me.

Each tear, each shout, a necessary part
Of mending the fractures deep in my heart.
For healing is messy, it's tangled and hot,
But it's in these moments, growth is sought.

So, I stir the pot, let the emotions flow.
Embrace the chaos, let the feelings show.
But, baby! **I'm human, a work in progress**, so true.
So, don't tempt me, I'm striving to renew.

REFLECTIONS & REVELATIONS

DATE:

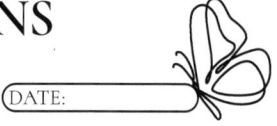

Journal Reflection:

- Reflect on a time when you allowed yourself to fully experience your emotions. How did embracing the chaos help you in your healing journey?
- What are the steps to healing, in your perspective, and how do you move from chaos to growth?

Discussion Questions:

- How do you personally embrace the "messiness" of healing? Are there specific emotions or actions that help you through the process?
- What areas of your life do you feel are still a 'work in progress,' and what steps are you taking to continue healing and growing?

_____

_____

_____

_____

_____

_____

_____

_____

_____

TRUST THE PROCESS

THE HEALING CYCLE

Healing comes in ripples— not a straight line.
No easy way, no shortcut in time.
You heal, you feel, you experience the pain.
A trigger appears, you heal once again.

It's a cycle, relentless and can feel unkind.
Each wave brings a lesson, a piece of your mind.
The hurt resurfaces, tears might flow,
But each time you rise, each time you grow.

Feel the depth of every ache.
Embrace the process for your own sake.
Experience the sorrow, the joy, the despair,
Each emotion, a step, taking you there.

Healing is messy, tangled, and raw,
But with each cycle, you rebuild, you soften and thaw.

No easy way, but a journey profound.
In the waves of healing, your power is found.
So heal, feel, experience and endure.
For in this cycle, your inner joy finds its cure.

SHE FINALLY WOKE THE FUCK UP

BREAKING NEWS: SHE FINALLY WOKE THE FUCK UP!

One morning, she stirred from her slumber with an unfamiliar clarity. Was this the moment she had been waiting for? It wasn't just a single event but a culmination of moments and experiences that had subtly built up during her nights. Could these be shouts of her soul, trailing up and down her spine, sometimes twisting it, other times aligning it perfectly?

When she finally opened her eyes, why did a profound sense of peace wash over her, cascading from the crown of her head to the tips of her toes? She leaped from her slumber. Her back felt transformed. Standing before the mirror, did her posture seem more grounded and unyielding than ever before? Surprisingly, she didn't reach out for her glasses, yet the world appeared sharper than ever before. How could this be?

She felt a deep sense of realization; she understood that she was a melody, a force, a gift. But was she a prized possession or a token to be flaunted? Or was she a beacon of light and potential? This realization wasn't rooted in arrogance but in a profound understanding of her worth and the unique energy she brought to the world. Could it be that she had faced trials and tribulations, yet each one had polished her, refined her, and made her shine even brighter?

Today, with renewed vision and strength, did she grasp the purpose of her journey? She was here not just to exist but to inspire, to touch lives, and to be a living testament to resilience and grace. Was she indeed a gift to the world and herself? For far too long, she had envisioned who she was in the wrong way, but that's okay. She's got it now.

Is this what it means to finally wake the fuck up?

The magic you seek lies in unseen deeds.
The dreams you chase are unplanted seeds.
In the limbo of procrastination, true magic hides. In tasks left undone, it's where your potential resides.
Open your arms to the challenge, let persistence be your guide
For in the work you're avoiding, your true power resides.

REFLECTIONS & REVELATIONS

DATE:

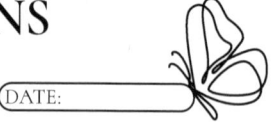

Journal Reflection:

- Make a list of things you've been avoiding in your relationships. How might addressing them help improve the connection?
- Think of a time you confronted an issue you'd been avoiding in a relationship. What changed afterward?

Discussion Questions:

- What are some 'unplanted seeds' in your relationships? What holds you back from nurturing them?
- How can avoiding difficult conversations or actions in relationships hide your potential for growth?
- How do you see the connection between effort and finding strength in your relationships?

_____
_____
_____
_____
_____
_____
_____
_____
_____

THE SHIFT

Change is natural — a course we cannot fight,
But when the path grows darker,
we lose sight.

I reach for you, but my hands return cold,
Realizing some battles aren't mine to hold.

The tracks have shifted, our journey has gone askew,
It's no one's fault, just what life sometimes will do.

Now you must choose if our worlds can realign,
Or if we leave the past in a place we can't find.

A MESSAGE

Rise with the dawn, carrying a fierce determination in your heart:
to accept nothing for yourself that you wouldn't desire for your daughters,
for you, too, are the precious child of someone's hopes and dreams.

CLARITY'S RELEASE

She walked the paths where darkness smiled.
A heart once open, freely given,
Under skies less stormy, more forgiven.

She loved a man, oh fiercely so,
But his heart marched to a drumbeat slow.
In his gaze, she saw not her reflection,
But a mirage of faint affection.

Power she found in a whispered word—*"Enough."*
No chains of longing, no binds of tough.
By stepping back, she cleared the view,
Gave him the space to see her anew.

For oft in closeness, we lose the sight
Of treasures held and worth the fight.
When she declared her final stand,
Let go the dream she once had planned,
It's then he sees, only an empty space,
The remnants of her, vanished without a trace.

WASTING TIME

The sand slips slowly through the glass.
With each grain, my angst grows fast.
I'm here with you, but I know inside,
The love I had for you has died.
Respect has faded, honor gone,
You were my choice, now it all feels wrong.
You squandered it, the bond we shared,
Now I'm here, my heart impaired.
I share this space, but my soul's away,
Tucked safely where you can't betray.
Right in front of you, I choose to stay,
In constant agony, wasting away.
Why don't I leave? Why do I stay?
The love I had, long stripped away.
I worry no longer if you stray,
Never my protector, only my damager—

**God deliver me from this turmoil,
self-inflicted, I desperately pray.**

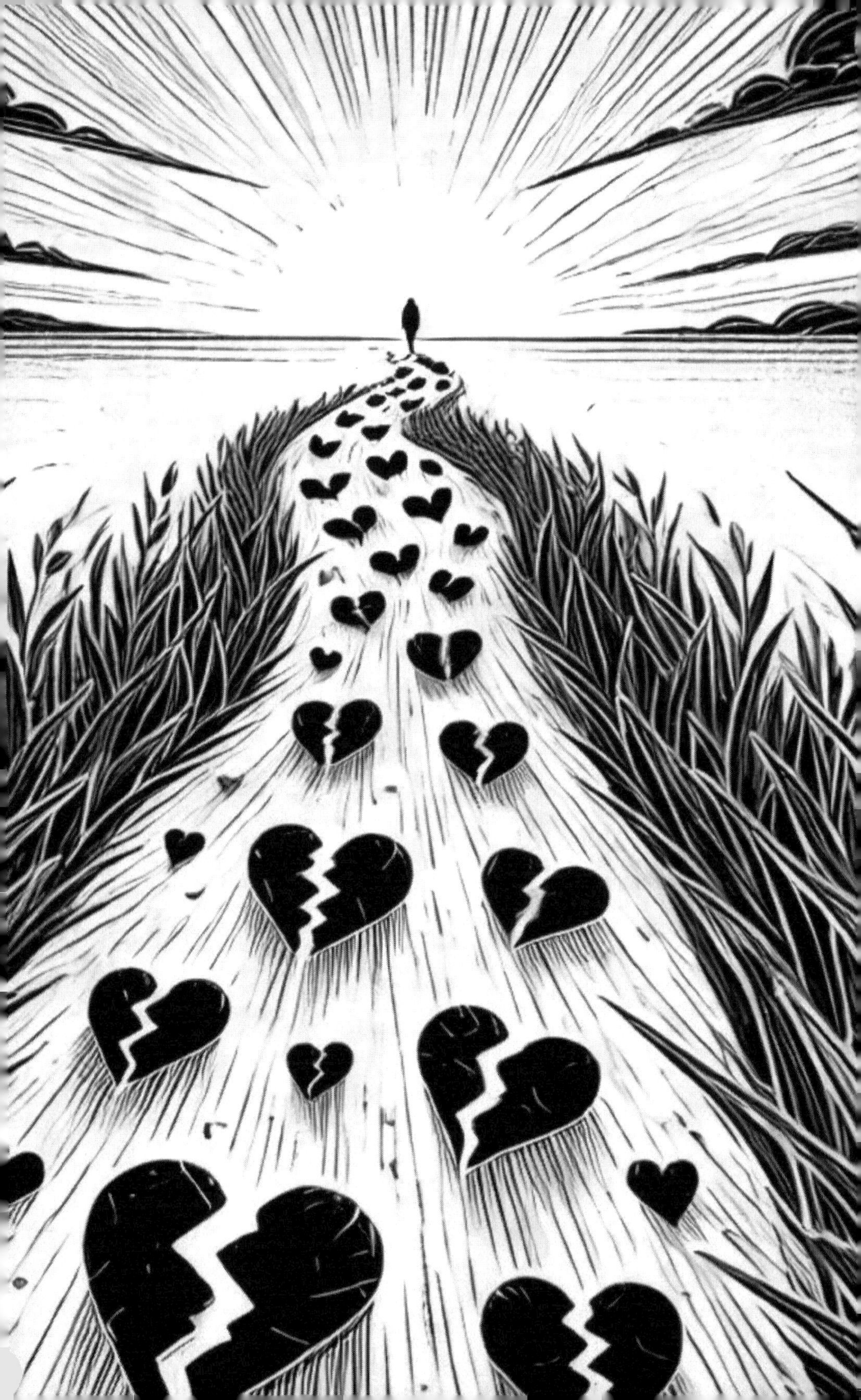

GONE BEFORE I LEFT

I left you long before my feet stepped out,
Drifted far, though I stayed close.
The words between us lost their weight,
as your constant lies suffocate,
In crowded rooms, I sat alone,
My thoughts no longer shared with you,
The quiet felt like sweet relief,
In silence, I knew we were through.
I stopped reaching, stopped the fight for us,
Let arguments dissolve to air,
Not out of peace, but out of loss,
Of caring if you were still there.
Each day, I lived two separate lives—
The one you saw, the one I kept.
Yes, I lived a life you couldn't see,
Hiding from who we ceased to be.
The smiles we wore were tired masks,
The simplest conversation, a giant task.
I'd long since slipped beyond your grasp,
The heart you squandered now in the past.

Gone before I left, it's true,
I mourned the man I thought was you.
You thought you had me under a stupid spell,
Silently hoping to drag my soul to hell,
But darling, here's the final blow—
You were finished long before I told you so.

REMEMBER AND FORGIVE

Access to me, more than likely, will be denied,
I will never see you the same, however I tried.
Releasing resentment, shielding my heart with care,
Boundaries set firm; in the fresh air I dare.

I grant this forgiveness, because it's not just for you,
It frees my soul too, lets light filter through.
I now know I never needed your sorry to be said,
Nor acknowledgement of the hurt that you spread.

I waited for you to fix me, to make me feel whole,
But that was my error, relinquishing control.
What I needed was to give myself permission to heal,
To mend my own spirit, to begin to feel real.
For peace is a choice, and love is the key,
In letting go, I finally set myself free.
I wish you the best, as we part, you and I,
On paths diverged under the same sky.

Write this down: *Forgiveness is a profound act of liberation!*

REFLECTIONS & REVELATIONS

DATE:

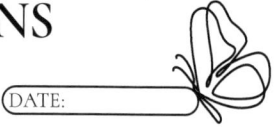

Journal Reflection:

- What does forgiveness look like for you when it's more about freeing yourself than the other person?
- Have you ever waited for an apology that never came, and how did you move forward?
- What boundaries do you set once you've forgiven someone, but you're still keeping your guard up?

Discussion Questions:

- Do you believe in "forgive and forget," or do those memories always linger?
- What's the hardest part of forgiving someone, even when they don't deserve it?
- How do you balance forgiving others while still protecting yourself from future hurt?

_____
_____
_____
_____
_____
_____
_____
_____

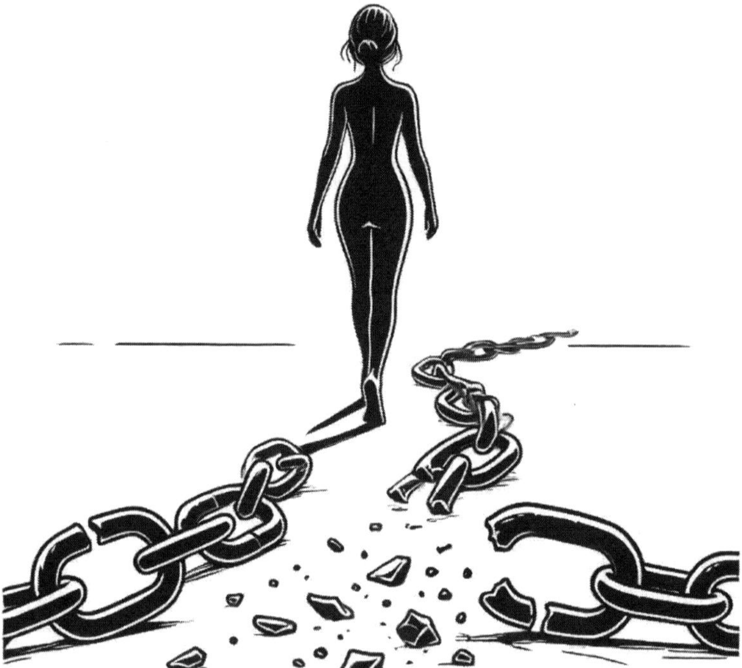

BREAKING MOTHER'S CHAINS

Yearning for more, a soul aching to be free?
But hark, dear daughter, listen close,
To the whispers of your heart, as it arose.
Love knows no boundaries, nor sets limits true.
It should lift you high, and make your spirit anew.
You deserve affection, shared with care,
A love that blossoms, a love that's rare.

Break the chains that confine your soul,
Embrace your worth, and let your heart be whole.
For in your footsteps, your mother resides,
A legacy of strength, deep within your tides.
It's time to break free, let your spirit soar,
To find a love that's worth fighting for.

For you, dear daughter, deserve to see,
A love that's real, and sets you free.
You deserve the stars, the moon, and the sea,
A love that's true, unequivocally.

Follow your heart, with strength and belief,
Forge a path where love brings only relief.
In your mother's footsteps, you need not stay,
Break free from the darkness, light up your way.
The journey is daunting, but you'll find your place,
In a love that uplifts, with joy and grace.
I wish my mother had told this to me,
To break the cycle, my sweet, and be free.

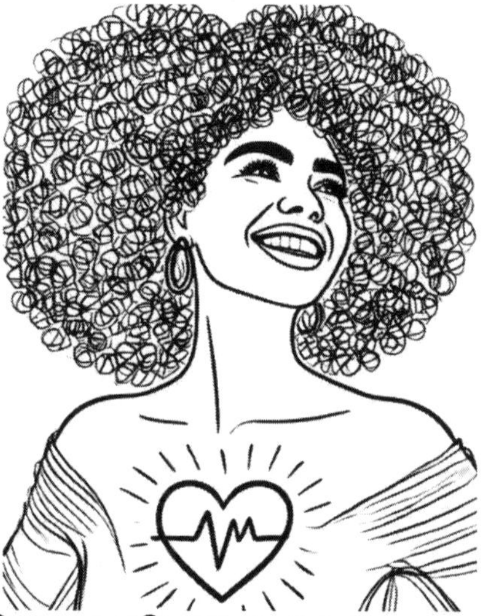

NON-NEGOTIABLE

There are non-negotiable standards to loving me. I am flawfully unapologetic, yet willing to be seen. I bare my soul, in hopes of joy and glee, to find the one who embraces all I've been.

I will not allow someone who fumbled my heart, to lead me to believe true love isn't waiting for me. With steadfast hope, I'll play my part, knowing that genuine love is my destiny.

I love life, needing it to consume me whole, excited to march to my own drumbeat's song. Alone or in unison, I honor my soul. In this dance of life, I know where I belong.

I accept and acknowledge all the experiences I've faced, The inflammation in my joints, the ache in my heart. Those cracks in my soul? Healed. Their lines traced, pathways to my peace, with joy, life, and healing as my art.

Non-negotiable standards guide my way. Embracing love and light, come what may.

REFLECTIONS & REVELATIONS

DATE:

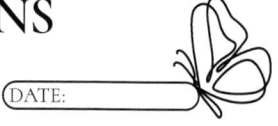

Journal Reflection:

- Make a list of your non-negotiables in love and relationships.
- How do they help you protect your sense of self?
- Reflect on a time when you felt fully seen and accepted in a relationship. How did it impact your connection?

Discussion Questions:

- What are your non-negotiable standards when it comes to being loved and accepted in a relationship?
- How important is it for you to feel fully seen and embraced, flaws and all, by your partner?
- What does being 'flawfully unapologetic' about who you are look like in your relationships? How do you balance this with growth?

_____
_____
_____
_____
_____
_____
_____
_____

FLIRTING OR RAISED RIGHT?

I've been off the market so long, now a question blooms:
Is he courting, or merely kind in these rooms?
His manners so gentle, his nurture so bright.
Is it fondness that stirs, or just doing what's right?
I ponder and waver, in his warmth, I bask.
Is there meaning behind that considerate mask?
Each gesture and smile, so perfectly cast.
Is it flirtation at play, or politeness that's vast?
In the web of his kindness, I cautiously tread,
Searching for signs in each word that he said.
I pull back, unsure, in this intricate rite,
Is he flirting, or was he just raised right?

MY DEAREST NEXT LIFETIME LOVE

I find myself next to him penning this ode to you. It's a testament to a bond that transcends the mere confines of time and circumstance. In you, I have discovered not just a friend but the aspiration for a future love that stirs my soul with a profound sense of hope and possibilities.

Your presence is a sanctuary where my spirit finds peace. You walk through life with a drive and an ethical compass that not only protects but enriches my heart and those around you. In your company, I journey through a world where I can lower my guards and breathe relaxed, unshackled by the burdens of self- defense.

You, who stand taller, meet me at the level of my eyes, embracing the depths of me without fear. You do not shrink from my greatness nor chide my flaws. Instead, you celebrate my entirety, encouraging my light to shine unfiltered. Your love, poured freely into the well of my being, seeks no reward—it simply seeks to quench the magic of our intertwined spirits.

Our reality dictates that we remain merely friends. This bond suffices for now, for it has shown me the true essence of reciprocal love. You have proven that my yearnings for deep connection and understanding are tangible possibilities, not mere flights of fancy.

I vow to seek you again in another life, where perhaps the stars may align, illuminating our paths and allowing them not just to cross and merge. Until then, I cherish the invaluable lessons of love and acceptance you have gifted me in this lifetime.

Thank you, my dearest friend, for this glimpse of what awaits us beyond the mask of the now.

With all the love that transcends time,
Me

REFLECTIONS & REVELATIONS

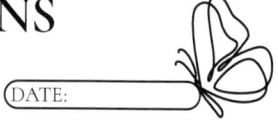

DATE:

Journal Reflection:

- Reflect on a friendship or relationship that profoundly impacted you but couldn't become romantic. How did it shape your understanding of love and connection?
- How does experiencing a deep emotional connection with someone, even if it remains just a friendship, influence your view of future relationships?

Discussion Questions:

- How does this poem explore the balance between friendship and romantic feelings? Have you ever experienced a similar bond?
- What does it mean to be truly seen and celebrated by someone?
- How do you navigate relationships where the connection feels deep, but circumstances prevent it from becoming more?

MY SOUL'S PROMISE TO ME

Dear Self,

I must confess that my heart is still tethered to another—a ghost from a previous chapter I'm working hard to close. As I pen this letter to you, my spirit has a profound sense of urgency mingled with a gentle patience. I acknowledge the need for healing, not rushed or forced, but undertaken with the care and tenderness it deserves.

I promise to embark on this journey of recovery, to nurture our wounded parts, and to afford us the time necessary for true healing. Let's not be swayed by the pressure to 'get over it' or 'move on' quickly. Healing, like growth, is a process that cannot be expedited without consequences.

As we venture through this healing process, I pledge to be kind to us, to be understanding of our setbacks, and to celebrate our small victories. I promise to listen to our needs, to rest when we are tired, and to push forward when we have the strength. I will honor our pace, and march to our own drumbeat, no matter how slow it might seem to the outside world.

Remember, the ghost that haunts us now will one day become a mere shadow in the light of our recovery. Each step we take is a step away from the past and toward a new chapter—one filled with hope, self-love, and newfound peace.

With all the compassion and commitment,
I can muster,
ME

REFLECTIONS & REVELATIONS

DATE:

Journal Reflection:

- Write your own soul promise—a personal commitment to yourself for healing and self-growth. What do you need to release or nurture in this promise?
- Reflect on a past relationship that you're still tethered to. What steps can you take to gently close that chapter and focus on your healing?

Discussion Questions:

- How do you navigate the process of closing a chapter with someone who still holds a part of your heart?
- What role does patience play in the healing process, and how do you find balance between urgency and self-care??

ABOUT THE AUTHOR

Step into the enchanting world of Laurel E. Moorehead-Suarez, a native of the sun-kissed paradise of St. Croix, U.S. Virgin Islands, where the vibrant flow of her imagination weaves tales that will captivate your heart and mind. From the tender age of 3, Laurel discovered her insatiable passion for reading and literature, sparking a lifelong affair with the written word and the magic of storytelling.

Immersed in the pages of countless books, Laurel's love for literature blossomed, and she found herself drawn to the art of storytelling like a moth to a flame. It wasn't long before she began to nurture her own creativity, crafting intricate narratives that breathed life into fascinating characters and compelling worlds. As she grew, so did her storytelling prowess, and the boundless possibilities of her imagination knew no bounds.

Beyond her enchanting tales, Laurel's life is a mosaic of devotion, love, and inspiration. She finds the inspiration for her stories in the laughter, tears, and triumphs of her family's journey. They are her constant companions, driving her to create stories that resonate deeply with readers of all ages. But Laurel's passions extend beyond the realm of storytelling. She is a visionary educator with a career spanning over 25 years, dedicating her time and expertise to shaping the landscape of education. Armed with a Master's degree in Education, Laurel's commitment to change led her to establish Compass Outreach and Education Center, Croix Management Group, and CompassPointe MicroSchool Solutions. She also owns Flawfully Unapologetic, where she tells stories through the candles she creates.

www.laurelthewriter.com | www.flawfully.com

OTHER BOOKS BY LAUREL

NILA'S SEASONS
SECRETS FROM THE ATTIC

As Ava delves into her mother Nila's journal, she uncovers revealing insights that shed light on hidden aspects of her family dynamics and the deliberate choices that led her mother to engage in a seasonal dance with infidelity.

MAJOR AND EMILIA'S
ISLAND ADVENTURE

Set Out On A Thrilling Mystery- Filled Adventure And Take On the Role Of A Detective Alongside Major and Emilia As They Solve The Case Of The Hungry Burglar!

You can find them on www. laurelthewriter.com

Made in the USA
Columbia, SC
30 November 2024